THE Rhythm

THE Rhythm

BEING YOUR BEST IN SPORT AND BUSINESS

RICHARD LONETTO, Ph.D.

Doubleday Canada Limited, Toronto

Canadian Cataloguing in Publication Data

Lonetto, Richard, 1942-
    The rhythm: being your best in sport and business

ISBN 0-385-25105-X

1. Success in business.   2. Sports – Psychological aspects.   3. Attention.
I. Title.

HF5386.L66 1988   650   C88-093059-4

DESIGN: Brant Cowie/Artplus Limited
Printed and bound in Canada

Published in Canada by
Doubleday Canada Limited
105 Bond Street
Toronto, Ontario
M5B 1Y3

All attempts have been made to contact the copyright holders in order to clear permission for material used in this book. In the event that the publishers have inadvertently overlooked a reference would the copyright holders please contact the Toronto office.

Dedication

THIS BOOK IS dedicated to the athletes, coaches, managers, officials, teams, and businesspeople who so graciously gave of their time, interest, and enthusiasm: George Knudson, Lorne Rubenstein, Jim Nelford, Dick Zokol, Blaine McCallister, Ralph Fiske, John Marshall, Bruce Hood, John D'Amico, Gary Green, Roger Neilson, Bob Lemieux, Dave Moote, Iain Douglas, Heather Kemkaran, Dick Brown, Garney Henley, Dave Lane, Jim Mossup, Mark Brown, Brad Hall, Fred Dunbar, Father David Bauer, Fred Shero, Billy Harris, Boris Kulagin, Peter Elson, Stewart O'Brien, Mike Barnett, Eddie Cardieri, Tom Treblehorn, Gordon Ash, Victor Regalado, Bill Britton, Janet Coles, Barbara Bunkowsky, Peter Nicholson, John Tory, Christine Marks, Andre Bordeleau, Philip Clarke, Ramji Sonji, the University of Guelph Football, Basketball, and Ice Hockey Teams, the Kalamazoo Wings Hockey Club, the American Ice Hockey League, the Brampton Ice Hockey League, the Ontario Amateur Hockey Association, and the College of Chiropractic Sports Sciences (Canada).

Contents

Introduction

H E LOVED BEING there. It was an awareness that he used beyond sport. His life had changed as he experienced the profound cycles of excitement, the wonder of feeling timeless, and the pleasures of release. He knew others had experienced it in their lives — but he worked at it; they didn't. They thought it was a magical gift. It wasn't. It was practice for both the mind and body that got him where he wanted to be. Practicing each alone wouldn't do it. When mind and body worked as one, there was no fear, only a sweeping insight into what he could do.

He stood, leaning against the wind, letting its noise surround him. He was shifting his thoughts, getting ready to be quiet so he could see into the future. He had to perform in a few minutes. When he was a child, it had all come so easily. Now he had to make it look easy for the spectators. He was being paid an enormous amount of money to be a professional athlete. Yet, all he wanted right then was a moment of quiet, a relief from the tension, a return to a time when he was young. He knew instinctively how to do it. For an instant, he could hear the shouting. They wanted to be part of it. Instead of being quiet and feeling what it was like, they distracted him. They also watched and studied his movements.

He allowed himself to feel their presence, but only for the briefest time. This was his way of testing himself. Sometimes, their demands were a burden that tired him,

1

made his legs heavy and his arms graceless appendages. Gradually, he quieted them in his mind until he could neither see or hear them. Then, he quieted himself and gentled the noise of the wind. Some of his friends could play a better technical game, had better swings, better moves, but he had a better mind. Over the years, his mind became an ally, a trusted companion. That's what made him a professional.

The greater the crowds, the more alone he became. The more strangers around him, the more he knew himself. Now, all he wanted to do, needed to do, was to be still — to feel the flow of his thoughts through his body and on out into the space around him. He waited for the feeling of timelessness that would come to mark the boundary that joined his thoughts to his actions. In this moment he was ageless and powerful. After this moment, he could play a game that few could match.

He had been there before, many times before. By now he had learned to trust himself there. By competing against himself, his greatest opponent, he had come to respect and recognize the value of being still before acting. He also knew that he could conceal this movement from others. The only clue they might pick up was a soft smile and laugh after he had acted.

He could lose the feeling and return to it again. When he was anxious, unsure, it was lost and he became mechanical. It was also lost when he tried to control it too much, or when he forgot about his natural rhythms.

When he lost the stillness, he felt like a robot performing some endlessly repetitive job, like an inefficient machine. His hinges were slightly off-center, and his movements quick and erratic. It was an awful experience to be robbed of fluid movement, of the ability to be totally involved in what he was doing. He hated the feeling of being in pieces, disconnected from his true nature, and still having to perform.

But because he was a professional, he could retrieve it when he needed it.

He didn't have the words for it, but he understood that it was a time unlike any other time in his life. Here, he could move effortlessly, be part and not part of the world at the same time, be in motion and still. Here, everything was so simple and made so much sense. Everything was absolutely right.

He was never in awe of this feeling because he had come to know it well. It was an experience that made him feel completely whole. If the music was there, his mind and body could merge in a universal stillness. Then, he could be the best. It was so simple and peaceful.

Achieving Mastery: The Rhythm

MANY OF THE serious, and not so serious, problems in our lives are not due to lucky or unlucky events we've experienced or to mistakes we've made, but have to do with the way in which we deal with our problems. In particular, the way we prepare ourselves, make decisions, and take action reflects the way we see events in the world around us and interact with them. When preparation, decision-making, and action are in harmony, when you can actually feel them effortlessly flowing one into the other, you will know what it is like to achieve mastery over yourself and the outside world.

This is what being in Rhythm is all about: to be effective and successful; to be able to commit yourself fully to a course of action, follow it through, and then be ready for a new challenge. In the pages to follow you will see what this Rhythm looks like and feels like, and learn how to use it in all aspects of your life. Your natural Rhythm is a blend of intellect, intuition, and mechanics that is designed to produce the best outcome possible. It is a state of mind that gives you the opportunity to succeed time and time again. It is a personal formula that you can feel, manage, and strengthen.

For over 12 years, I have studied and worked with athletes of both sexes, from rank beginners to elite amateurs and professionals, in such sports as golf, ice hockey, football, figure skating, shooting, basketball, baseball, tennis, and squash. The idea behind this work was to develop ways in which athletes, coaches, and managers could control their tension and anxiety, and perform at a consistently high level. I wanted to provide each person with a method that he or she could use to achieve a better understanding of how to act under pressure. This work also attracted the attention of businesspeople, who saw how the benefits of better self-management, particularly under pressure, could translate in the work place.

What I found took me by surprise for two reasons: I wasn't looking for it; and it was so simple and worked so well that I could easily have overlooked it. No matter what the activity, no matter what the experience or skill level of each man or woman, boy or girl, there was a recurring pattern that appeared whenever their performance was successful. This pattern involved the heart rate and/or respiration and for all practical purposes, was identical for a golfer who had been hitting balls for six to eight hours a day for years, and had to perform while people all over the world watched; a businessperson trying to manage a long iron or a problem at work; and a parent deciding how to deal with a problem at home. It is a cyclical wave-like pattern that I call *The Rhythm*. It has three interdependent stages beginning with preparation and ending in action, with a time of quiet and decisiveness bonding them together that I call the Trough of the Waves or the Still-Point. And the Rhythm can be recognized, understood, and managed by each of us.

Your Rhythm might be considered an experience equivalent to meditating and being active at the same time. But is isn't an altered state: it is your most natural state. It involves letting go and being in control at the same time, being decisive and trusting, strong and calm; and feeling that your actions will have a positive impact. In this "state" you are given the opportunity to look inside yourself and thus to experience a new vision of the world around you.

Rhythm . . . expresses itself as a flowing movement of one motion into another without any breaks. It is a feeling

*derived from a coordination of mind and muscle that
enables the player to do exactly the right thing at the proper
moment.*

[Modified from Percy Boomer, On Learning Golf, 1959, p. 155]

The Waves

ALL SYSTEMS HAVE within them a natural geometry. The
wave-like pattern of the Rhythm is its natural
geometry. It is your personal bio-system that tunes you to
your true self, and to past, present, and future events in the
world around you. It keeps you balanced and in harmony.
Your experience of the motions of these waves is direct and
immediate.

THE RHYTHM

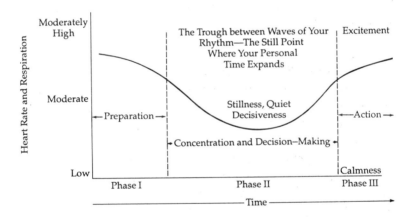

---

*These levels of heart rate and respiraton are relative, and have different
meanings for different men and women, However, their pattern of
change remains the same when they are in Rhythm.

The waves of your Rhythm begin with the excitement of
preparation and end with the release of energy into action.
The phases of these waves blend into each other and are
distinguishable by your personal experience.

Your Rhythm follows the basic, unchangeable laws of the human condition. It is a secret that each of us can discover and utilize. It is the experience of a continuing harmony between mind and body, a trust in what you can accomplish, and contains the knowledge that you can be both compassionate and successful. As you recognize and use your Rhythm, you will appreciate its apparent paradoxes — that you can be relaxed and strong, and let go and be in control at the same time.

Harmony between mind and body is not an esoteric idea, or an unrealistic goal; it is absolutely necessary if you want to develop and combine your personal strength with compassion. Once you establish this bond, it cannot be broken. It will feel so simple that you will have to laugh at yourself for thinking it was so complex. This is the laughter of personal enlightenment. It is the knowledge that simple things cannot be easily damaged or reduced, while complicated things break down far more easily and often. This feeling of simplicity is a perfect reflection of your Rhythm.

Being out of Rhythm also has a distinctive pattern. It is not flowing or wave-like; instead, as the figure on page 7 shows, it is a line that tends to rise from the excitement of beginning a task to the anxiety of never seeing it done properly or at all. This pattern is a reflection of a lack of cohesion, of being in pieces, of things slipping away, and of being frustrated at every turn. The rising line begins to collapse as fatigue and exhaustion set in, along with a sense of urgency because you now have to make up for lost time. Your preparation was lost because you were too anxious and tense to make a good decision and act on it. Now, everything has to be rushed because there is less time to do any one thing. When tension and stress are permitted to straighten out your Rhythm, they take the essential character of your personality with it. The trough between the waves is gone; its stillness turns to anxiety, and later to turbulence. This alteration in your Rhythm can be experienced as a neurotic cycle that leads to an inability to make decisions and act on them.

BEING OUT OF RHYTHM

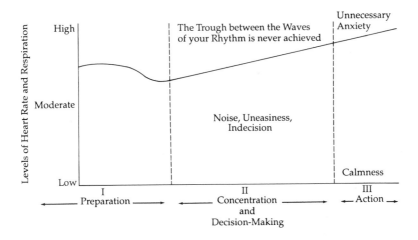

Each of us has felt this pattern, but how many of us believe that it can be controlled? I am absolutely convinced that it can. As you go through this book and do the exercises in each chapter, you will be teaching yourself how to do it. There are no mysteries here. Your Rhythm is a natural guide to successful thought and action; you just have to learn how to trigger it and maintain it.

Phase II of your Rhythm is the time in which everything feels as if it falls into its proper place. Your thinking is crystal clear, your decisions focused and correct. The actions that follow will seem to flow as if they are inseparable pieces of the same whole. This moment is not a gift that is given by others. This moment is yours. It is a "sweet spot" in your life. Some researchers have called it part of your "flow," a state only reached by elite athletes. They are wrong! Throughout this book, I will be reminding you just how natural it is to be the best you can be, and to feel good about what you are thinking and doing.

Oriental schools of philosophy, politics, and commerce have been built on principles emphasizing the natural and productive side of our character, while in Europe and North America, outside the years of childhood, sport and physical activity have been our ways of joining our natural feelings and thoughts with action. In other words, what meditation has been to the East, sport is to the West. We are finally beginning to appreciate and understand the amazing variety of effects these activities can have on our lives, and what we learn about ourselves through physical activity can easily be transfered to other parts of everyday life. *Whether you are playing or working, concentration on what you are doing strengthens you.*

This means that putting a golf ball in your office, playing a game with your children, doing something you like, or even washing the dishes or the car can actually improve your mind and body. For over a decade I have seen and experienced what the Rhythm can do.

What are the benefits of staying in Rhythm and using it when you have to? First of all, you are a better manager of yourself, and this means you trust yourself to get out of your own way and *let your thinking do your thinking.* Second, when you are in this frame of mind, you cannot do things half-way or be indecisive. Finally, one of the greatest benefits is that you will come to realize that you can be relaxed and in complete control at the same time.

All of these benefits translate into better performance: after going through the exercises I set out in this book, goaltenders reduced their goals-against average by 8% to 17%; shooters, quarterbacks, and pitchers improved their accuracy by 5% to 9%; a basketball team set a tournament record by hitting 63 of 65 free-throws; professional golfers reduced their stroke average enough to triple their previous earnings. Weekend and noncompetitive athletes improved their performance on the field and at work; and businesspeople made better and more effective decisions without the usual anxieties and frustrations.

Sports and business have more in common than many of us imagine. Numerous athletes have made the switch from the playing field to the boardroom: in both arenas, success depends on effective and efficient decision-making and action. To be effective in sport requires a harmony between thought and action, between mind and body, that becomes a distinct and identifiable Rhythm. By applying the same principles to your work, you can also achieve success.

The interplay between sport and business means that you can strengthen your decision-making abilities by practicing and playing your favorite sport instead of spending time in an over-air-conditioned seminar room. By understanding yourself, reaching the trough in the waves of your Rhythm in the sport or activity of your choice, you strengthen your ability to reach the same point in your office, at home, or anywhere your have to make an important or everyday decision. In the trough you will find the "trigger" point of making your decisions — the "turning" point where action begins.

> *The greatest skill seems like pure simplicity.*
> *[The* Tao Te Ching *XLV, quoted in Juan Mascaró,* Lamps of Fire.
> *1972, p. 176]*

The Chapters

I N EVERYTHING we do or think, there is a pattern. In this book, each chapter is complete in itself while at the same time it mirrors the entire book. Each of the chapters represents a shift in perspective so you can rediscover and strengthen your ability to use your inner Rhythm. Keep an open mind as you go through the book. Don't be too accepting of the things you already feel are true, or reject the presence of things you haven't yet explored.

The exercises throughout the book were designed so that you can be your own teacher, and learn in a way that makes the most sense to you. No one knows better than you what you are feeling and thinking, and what you want to accomplish. By being your own teacher, you will learn all the secrets you need to know. They will come to you; you won't have to look for them. There really is a best way for each of us, and we can find it for ourselves if we let our natural intellectual and intuitive powers guide us. Chapter 1 describes certain of these powers: the secrets of control and of slowing down. This chapter also introduces an es-

sential preparatory exercise — one that the book draws on
consistently: learning to close your eyes.

Chapters 2, 3, and 4 detail each mutually interdependent
phase of the Rhythm. You will start by developing
strategies to ensure that your Preparation will lead to a
time of quiet decisiveness. You will learn to experience
stillness and to gain complete control before "letting yourself go" to act. The change from stillness into action is the
last phase of the complete cycle of the Rhythm. This is
where your preparation and quiet control are transformed
into effective action. The excercises in Chapter 4 will give
you the experience of feeling the change while learning
how to use it. I've found that it generally takes from three
to five days to establish a good basis for realizing and understanding your Rhythm. By this time, you will have uncovered the personal "triggers" and "rituals" that set your
Rhythm into motion.

Now you can begin to fine-tune your Rhythm, and
Chapters 5 and 6 were designed to give you a start in that
direction. Chapter 5 focuses on improving your ability to
concentrate, its connection to moments of inspiration, and
the myths that surround the discipline of begin able to
concentrate. For example, you only have to concentrate for
a few minutes each day to be successful. The trick is to
know which minutes, and by using the exercises in the
chapter, you will be better able to locate them. Chapter 6
outlines the secret of managing time; you'll learn how to
save spending any more time or money on workshops.
Once you begin to understand the way time can be used to
your benefit, you can make better predictions about the
imminent future and stop trying to be in two places at
once. In particular, you can stop trying to see how things
will turn out before you've even begun. A brief history of
our attempts to capture and measure time is included in
Appendix C.

Using your Rhythm and maintaining it requires practice,
and Chapter 7 provides guidelines for doing that. You will
be practicing in a new way, one that combines mechanics
with thoughts and feelings. This is the kind of exercising

that shortens the walk from practice to play, leaving behind unnecessary tension and anxiety. Through this new
way of practicing, you will build up rituals to guarantee
that your Rhythm will be there when you need it.

At this point, you might want to put your Rhythm to a
further test. Appendix A includes a number of scales and
schedules that you can fill in to rate your levels of stress,
mood, and temper. Appendix B includes the instructions
for a Decision-Making Game that you can play over and
over. The game shows you the pattern of your decision-
making strategies, and how it shifts over time until you
reach a decision. It is a personal record of how you
prepared, decided, and took action.

1 *Real Secrets*

Changing for the Better

HOW MUCH DOES performance have to change to be successful? Most of us tend to have an exaggerated idea about the nature of these changes: answers of about 10% to 20% or more seem common. Surprisingly, however, changes on the order of 1% to about 5% can bring about extraordinary success. If a baseball team shaved about 4% to 5% from its pitching staff's earned run average (e.r.a.), this could translate into as many as 15 to 20 more games won in a season. A 3% to 5% improvement in the free-throw shooting accuracy of a basketball team could mean an increase of 20 or more games in the win column. For a professional golfer, a reduction in stroke average of 1% to 3%, could make the difference between being one of the top 60 money winners and one of the top 10.

In business, improvements in concentration, decision-making, and subsequent actions of less than 5% could translate into highly visible and significant changes and gains, both personally and for the organization. As I mentioned in the introduction, the ability to recognize and use your Rhythm in sports translates easily and directly into your business, home, and social life. The Rhythm in your sport or favorite activity is identical to the one needed in any situation demanding concentration, decision-making, and action.

In the Orient it is not a radical idea that self-control learned through a physical activity (e.g., archery or various forms of the martial arts) opens the world to us in new and wondrous ways. What we can gain from Oriental approaches to learning are three basic and unalterable rules that, in our society, translate into success:

If you know yourself and the nature of the problem, you can be 100% successful. This is what using your Rhythm assures once you let it work for you.

If you know yourself, and not the nature of the problem, or vice versa, you can be only 50% successful.

If you don't know yourself and the nature of the problem, you cannot succeed. This is a life completely out of touch with its Rhythm.

North Americans and Europeans have tended to resist the use of meditation as a preliminary to action; yet in sport we have achieved a state in which meditation and performance are joined. In sport, many have experienced what it is like to be tranquil and perform well. This is what "coming through in the clutch" is all about — remaining calm while everything around you is noisy; making that impossible shot as if it were the easiest thing in the world. Through participation in your favorite activity, or one you want to learn, you will become aware of what triggers your Rhythm, and how to use it in other situations.

Real Secrets: Managing Yourself

It can happen to you. In a flashing moment something happens. . . . You see the same unsame world with fresh eyes.
[*Paul Reps*, Zen Flesh, Zen Bones, *p. 30.*]

REAL SECRETS ARE uncomplicated, simple, and extraordinarily useful. These secrets are tied to those moments of truth in your life when you realize that your present conflict is really a struggle against yourself. With this realization comes another secret: there is *a decision* you can make, and *an action* you can take with *integrity* and *compassion* that will also be *successful*. Any real secret has to contain all of these elements.

Secrets remind you of how strong you become when you are quiet and still, how you can stop limiting yourself by helping to take down the barriers in your way, and how good you can be at sensing an opportunity and seizing it. Secrets also unerringly return to one starting point:

YOU MUST FIRST LEARN HOW TO MANAGE YOURSELF BEFORE YOU CAN MANAGE ANYONE OR ANYTHING ELSE.

To manage yourself well means that you have to be able to experience and understand the inner patterns of your life, it rises and falls, its alternating speeds, and its path. This pattern is a wave-like cycle; to recognize its movements, to ride from its crests through its troughs and out again is to know *a personal secret*. For there is a characteristic pattern that unites mind and body to create a life without unnecessary tension — a life that blends together intellect, intuition, and decisiveness to create an action that is just and correct. This is a life that looks forward to the next task, that creates its own challenges and meaning.

Percy Boomer, once one of the most respected teachers in sport, once commented that in his 35 years of teaching golf, he had not found two people who played alike. No matter how much effort went into molding them to play similarly, the results were far from expected. Boomer's comments are even more relevant today, given the growing number of clinics, workshops, seminars, and schools designed to make you better at sports, in business, at home, or wherever you happen to be. The majority of these efforts seem to be aimed at making as many people as possible think and act alike, generally by teaching them to feel and act like a well-known athlete or businessperson.

Somewhere along the line, however, the individual who has to throw, hit, kick, run, swim, give a speech, or make an important decision that will affect others has been for-gotten. What has also been neglected is the fact that each of us sees the world in different ways, and we each have different abilities, temperaments, and needs. We keep signing up for these seminars and workshops because most of us, if not all of us, would really like to learn a secret — one that would change our lives for the better. False secrets can't do this for you, but they do give you a glimpse into those "sweet spots" in your life when every action was precise and flawlessly executed; when every thought was so radiant that it shattered anxiety and fears, producing an unusual calmness that seemed to stop time and then release you into the outside world. But as soon as this experience came, it passed. Your secret was somehow lost. The more you tried to recapture it, the farther away it moved, until it became no more than a memory or a dream. These false secrets only open the door a bit before it is closed again. It is your understanding and use of your own Rhythm that opens the doors completely and helps you to create your own sweet spot again and again. It's a practical formula that is meant to be used.

Secrets are false when they do not give you a way to understand, use and create. You know they are false because they leave behind a feeling of incompleteness and insecurity. On the other hand, the continually recurring pattern of the Rhythm will leave you with feelings of confidence and trust in yourself. You have much more control over your mental and physical states than you imagine! This is another secret, one beyond logic, that we all possess. It is the secret of control. In the pages and exercises to come, other personal secrets will be remembered. And the most basic one, your inner Rhythm, will show you how natural it feels to prepare, decide, concentrate, and act in a way that is right for you, and for others around you.

Real Secrets: Slowing Down

AS YOU PLAY, using the exercises throughout the book, you might discover some old secrets you can put to good use. The most basic secret is learning to trust yourself to do things all the way and not half-way. Another discovery may be that you learn to use your intuition as a guide to your decisions and actions. But there is one discovery that comes before all the others: you achieve what you want when you learn how to slow down. In learning to "be slow," there is power. This is the lesson of your Rhythm. Once you learn to recognize the different speed and time zones you can live in, you can pick the ones that work best for you.

LEARNING TO SLOW DOWN: *The Ring of Power*

> *The relationship between sensations, movements, and performance is a dynamic cycle. It is a personal cycle that is self-regulating and has a time structure of its own.*
> [*Georges Thinès*, Phenomenology and the Science of Behaviour,
> *1977, p. 53.*]

Power is lost when we become too fast. We may feel stronger, more in control. But these feelings are an illusion. Real power comes from learning to be slow. Real power comes from pacing oneself — from timing, not from speed. This is the "ring of power."

THE RING OF POWER

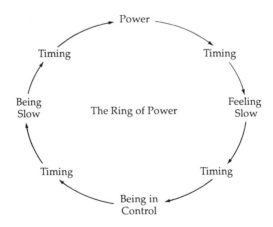

Too many people try to perform in a way that they feel will eliminate any errors due to distracting thoughts or negative emotions. Eliminating these errors means that the time gap between thought and action has to be erased, or greatly reduced. The faster they swing a golf club, baseball bat, or tennis or squash racquet, the less likely will time get in their way — or so they believe.

A pitcher told me that he had tried to "speed everything up" to reduce his anxiety and uncertainty. The time between getting the sign and actually throwing the ball caused this anxiety. So he reasoned that this time had to be eliminated. In doing so, he unravelled a once beautifully smooth and graceful motion, replacing it with a hurried one. His performance did not improve, but his anxiety did increase. Amateurs, even very good ones, usually don't give up their game entirely. On the other hand, they don't get any better, and instead become well acquainted with the effects of frustration.

More successful players, whether professional or amateur, and businesspeople do not speed up. They do just the opposite. They try to move more and more slowly, maintaining their timing, balancing their thoughts and actions. In actual game situations, or as a crucial game continues, they may seen to be even slower to observers. This is what "timing" or "pacing oneself" is all about. This is "being-in-Rhythm." This is the natural state that sets the stage for efficient and effective performance.

IT IS NATURAL TO LET YOUR FEELINGS WORK FOR YOU, NOT AGAINST YOU.

The strength of your game lies in the correct combination of mental attitude and physical abilities. *Your game* is a blend of good mechanics and beliefs about yourself. *Your timing* is felt as being able to be slow, quiet, and in control. The results will be powerfully efficient — this is *your edge,* your game as a reflection of you. A Roger Clemens fastball is a *fast ball.* Ingemar Stenmark can seem to navigate a slalom course more slowly than any competitor, yet have the fastest time. Jack Nicklaus, by just being in a tournament, can send waves through the whole course. Mikhail Baryshnikov, leaping and hovering in the air, has somehow altered the properties of gravity. Lee Iacocca's sense of timing and leadership has become legendary.

Each of us has a personal "ring of power." You have to learn how to use and trust yours. As you learn, you will see that power doesn't focus on results. It focuses on being in control of yourself.

Learning to Close Your Eyes

B EING SLOW AND quiet, trusting and feeling that you are in control, are continuing themes throughout this book. One way I have used over the past 12 years to give men, women, and children an idea of how they can produce these experiences for themselves is simply to have them close their eyes while they are doing something. This could be washing the dishes, walking around the house, kicking, hitting, or throwing a ball, swimming, running, even skiing.

Closing your eyes and having to be active at the same time makes you pay attention to yourself — the self that you can easily take for granted. How often have you taken yourself into account when you have to make a decision or are just playing? Often we look at ourselves but fail to see what is going on inside. I want you to "see," not just to "look." And, over time, I've found that by closing your eyes, you can do just that — you can see better! And, when you can see better, you are naturally in the right frame of mind when you open your eyes.

Doing things with your eyes closed that seem to defy common sense and ordinary expectations — e.g., pitching strikes, hitting a distant target — and then doing them with your eyes open builds your Rhythm and natural powers. In those exercises that you are asked to do with closed eyes, I've given you no choice but to depend on yourself. The links between mind and body are strengthened by performing with closed eyes. You and what you are doing gradually become one. There is no need to imagine what the outcome will be because you will naturally produce it. In spite of all the media attention given to the role of imagery in producing successful performances, there is no systematic body of evidence to prove it one way or the other. A mass of evidence, on the other hand, shows the relationship between imagination and performance to be tenuous, at the best of times. How many times have you performed well while you were thinking of all the disastrous things that could happen? Or played poorly while you imagined a brilliant result that would stun any audience? Or did something that you couldn't possibly imagine doing?

Imagery only works after you get to know yourself. No amount of positive imagery can help when you don't have the faintest idea how your inner states influence events and people in the world around you. However, once you know yourself and your inner Rhythm, almost anything can work for you. If you want to achieve true mastery, you have to know your Rhythm and how it works. You can't skip over this basic lesson.

You free yourself by closing your eyes to keep things simple and challenging. And I'll bet that most of you will hit longer and straighter, be faster and more accurate, after a few practice sessions with your eyes closed. Keep in mind that things are not always what they seem when your eyes are open.

EXERCISE 1:1 *Putting golf balls, throwing darts, riding an exercise bicycle, jogging in place, or doing sit-ups; washing dishes, vacuuming, taking a bath or shower — it doesn't really matter what activity you engage in: you are doing something that will help you understand your Rhythm. The next time you do one or more of these things in your office or at home, do it first for about 5 to 10 minutes with your eyes closed; then try it with your eyes opened. With your eyes closed, you will "feel" what you are doing: you will feel the ball move off the putter after sticking to it for a fraction of a second; you will feel your inner balance, your muscles at work; you will feel the target, and get a sense of where it is and how to get there; you will feel the coordinated movements of your body. When you open your eyes, you will see and feel with a new clarity that you can increase each time you do this simple exercise in everyday life.*

Provided he makes and wins an argument about Buddhism with those who live there, any wandering monk can remain in a Zen temple. If he is defeated, he has to move on.

In a temple in the northern part of Japan two brother monks were dwelling together. The elder one was learned, but the younger one was stupid and had but one eye.

A wandering monk came and asked for lodging, properly challenging them to a debate about the sublime teaching. The elder brother, tired that day from much studying, told the younger one to take his place. "Go and request the dialogue in silence," he continued.

So the young monk and the stranger went to the shrine and sat down.

Shortly afterwards the traveler rose and went in to the elder brother and said: "Your young brother is a wonderful fellow. He defeated me."

"Relate the dialogue to me," said the elder one.

"Well," explained the traveler, "first I held up one finger, representing Buddha, the enlightened one. So he held up two fingers, signifying Buddha and his teaching. I held up three fingers, representing Buddha, his teaching, and his followers, living the harmonious life. Then he shook his clenched fist in my face, indicating that all three came from one realization. Thus he won and so I have no right to remain here." With this, the traveler left.

"Where is that fellow?" asked the younger one, running in to his elder brother.

"I understand you won the debate."

"Won nothing. I'm going to beat him up."

"Tell me the subject of the debate," asked the elder one.

"Why, the minute he saw me he held up one finger, insulting me by insinuating that I have only one eye. Since he was a stranger I thought I would be polite to him, so I held up two fingers, congratulating him that he has two eyes. Then the impolite wretch held up three fingers, suggesting that between us we only have three eyes.

So I got mad and started to punch him, but he ran out and that ended it!"

[Paul Reps, Zen Flesh, Zen Bones, p. 10.]

2 The Crest of the First Wave: Preparation

EXCERCISE 2:1 *Before you begin to read this chapter, put on your favourite record or tape. Just let your thoughts pass and flow with the music for a few minutes. Then close your eyes for about 30 seconds and relax before you turn the page.*

THE RIGHT PREPARATION — *From Excitement to Calmness*

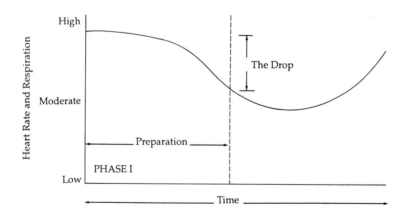

I N THE FIRST stage of the cycle of your Rhythm, you are riding on the crest of the first wave into the trough. You are preparing yourself to face a problem, whether it be a serve, a tee shot, waiting to give a speech or to go on stage, extinguishing your last cigarette, beginning a diet, or waiting to see the dentist. In this Preparation Phase, you are really trying to do two things at once: (1) process all the information that is available to you, including your feelings; and (2) will the outcome to turn out the way you want it to.

The process has to start that will bring the right pieces together. As you continue to look over the situation, you begin to calm down. At first you hardly notice the change; then, gradually, you do. This is such a common occurrence that you may have forgotten that this signals a moment of insight; a moment that initiates the process of Preparation. As you select the target you are shooting for, or bounce a ball in front of you, or make just one more note to yourself, you begin to feel calmer. Then, you feel "the drop." Your heart rate has slowed, and your breathing is hardly noticeable. This is another signal. This time it means that you are beginning to enter the next phase of the Rhythm — the area of the Still Point (see Chapter 3). You have to experience "the drop" or there will be no next phase, and no transition from preparation into action. Without "the drop" no decision can be made and acted on. This change has to be there and felt. If it isn't, you haven't prepared yourself properly to continue. Instead, what you have prepared the way for is a cycle of anxiety and poor performance.

Too often the outcome we want to achieve is lost because we get ourselves tangled up in thinking about the end before we've even begun. Successful men and women know from practice and experience that without care at the beginning there is no end. These men and women also appear to others to be in the *right place* at the *right time*. But this is only two-thirds of the story. They are not only in the right place and time; they are also in the *right frame of mind*. This last ingredient is what makes the place and time right. Being properly prepared combines your knowledge, skills, and intuition correctly and wisely. Being prepared is the only way you can ride over the crest, and in and out of the troughs of your Rhythm.

Being prepared is the first, and necessary, phase of the cycle that ends in success. If you have prepared properly, the result becomes a natural part of this preparation. Outcomes flow from the right preparation; they are not caused by them. This flowing relationship leads to feelings of confidence — sometimes overwhelming confidence.

> [J. Paul] Getty once received a request from a magazine for a short article explaining his success. A check for two hundred pounds was enclosed. The multimillionaire obligingly wrote: "Some people find oil. Other's don't."
> [Clifton Tediman (ed.), The Little, Brown Book of Anecodotes, 1985, p. 239]

To describe what it is like to be prepared, I will have to introduce a number of examples to help guide you to it and beyond.

Your club is leading by a run; the bases are loaded with one out in the bottom of the ninth. The other team's RBI leader is at the plate. You look in to get the sign. You are getting ready to begin your windup, but you're really not sure now if you picked the right pitch. What should you do now?

You are considering an offer that must be acted on by 3:00 p.m. and it's 1:30 p.m. Doubts begin to rise about the true value of this offer to your organization. But there is pressure on you from both sides to make a decision. You really can't put it off any longer. What can you do to deal with your doubts with so little time left?

Should you sell that stock your friends have told you about, or buy more as your broker suggests?

Your tee shot, on a 458-yard par 4 hole, has landed on the left side of the fairway. You're feeling pretty good today and have made some good shots. You have a chance to go for the green, but the green is heavily bunkered on the left side and you have always had trouble bringing the ball from left to right. Should you go for it?

Should you hire an applicant even though you still have doubts that others don't seem to have?

Each of these moments gives you the opportunity to bring your thoughts, feelings, and actions together to create what some call a "peak experience." During this experience, what you will achieve will seem effortless and absolutely right. But even if you do it this time, can you repeat it? You can — if you understand how you got there in the first place. To begin a cycle of your Rhythm, you have to prepare; then the other phases can take over. First, you have to practice and play to know the best preparation strategy for you, and what personal rituals are associated with it.

Those who know others are intelligent. Those who know themselves have insight. Those who master others have force. Those who master themselves have strength.

[R. L. Wing, The Tao of Power, 1986, p. 33]

EXERCISE 2:2 *Focus your attention at the instant your in-breath becomes an out-breath — the instant between the completion of inhaling and the beginning of exhaling. When you can do this, you will have touched a center of your tranquil energy. It is here that your thoughts are correct, as will be the decisions and actions that follow. This is the time to let your thoughts come to you. Stay still and give them a good target. You need to trust yourself here to let some things pass while others find you. Don't try to grab them. Stay calm. Try this exercise before you continue reading.*

Rituals

GETTING OUT of bed on the same side every day, putting your left shoe on before the right, making the light at Spruce Street, having coffee and Danish exactly at 10:20 a.m., smiling at Ms. Branson, preparing for a game of squash with Philip by arriving 15 minutes early so that you have enough time to calm down: these are the rituals of everyday life that we take so much for granted; but without them our days would not go as well.

For special days and events, there are other rituals: the suit or dress that comes out of protective hiding in the closet; that lucky tie or pair of shoes; the T-shirt you haven't changed in days because your team is on a winning streak; making sure you drive to the game along the same streets that have brought you victories in the past; taking your favorite seat in a restaurant, in a theatre, or at the ball park. These are all rituals designed to help you control events to come.

It has been said that "talent is the presence of the ability and the absence of understanding about the source and operation of knowledge" (Idries Shah, *Reflections*, 1972, p. 133). Great talent is the presence of the ability *and* the understanding. Highly successful athletes, executives, parents, and people know what their rituals are. They may not be able to articulate this precisely, but by watching them, you and I can see their rituals at work.

Fernando Valenzuela of the Dodgers rolling his eyes toward the sky as he delivers a pitch, and Robin Roberts of the Phillies winding his body up like a spring ready to throw, are examples of athletes with personal rituals. Wayne Gretzky of the Edmonton Oilers and Borje Salming of the Toronto Maple Leafs performing effortlessly, moving in a time that is different from the other players on the ice; Jack Nicklaus taking precisely the same time over every putt, knowing that this is part of his rhythm; and Tom Watson and Lee Trevino — each with a rhythm of his own visible to anyone watching them play a round of golf — are also examples. Willie Stargell tipping his bat and Jimmy Connors bouncing a tennis ball the same number of times before serving exhibit what some may call superstitious behavior, but these actions are really personal rituals to ensure the right preparation. These rituals work, as does wearing your favorite outfit for an important meeting or first date. Rituals help to keep your anxiety in check and "plug the possible leaks" in your concentration. Rituals serve as your personal signposts of the onset and end of a cycle of concentration, anticipation, and action. They make certain your preparation is perfectly tuned, and that you do not prepare longer than is necessary.

The traditional rituals in our society — those surrounding marriage, birth, and death — provide a framework for our emotions and thoughts. In the same way, our personal rituals keep our Rhythm in place so that we can concentrate and act. One of the first signals that our Rhythm is no longer there is that our ritual is no longer there either. I have found over the years that where anxiety is present, a fundamental piece of a person's pattern is missing — they have forgotten to use their rituals to keep them grounded. For a pitcher, a simple rocking motion of no more than six inches can be shortened or missing; for a golfer, a tightness in the neck and shoulders can throw off the alignment needed for a good shot, so that all of a sudden, the club doesn't feel right, and a long series of mechanical adjustments are made instead of only one.

Without knowing your ritual, you can spend an awful lot of time looking for mechanical solutions. Your ritual serves to release tension or hold it at bay until you have acted. *What is your ritual?* Think about the little things you do to cope with tension. If you can't think of any, ask some friends who have played with you what differences they notice in you when you are playing well and when you are playing poorly.

EXERCISE 2:3 *One ritual I use to gauge my tension level in tennis is to walk the court, before and during a match, from the net to the back court with my eyes closed. If I can stop right on the baseline, I know I'm fine. If I'm short, I know I'm tense; and if I'm long, I'm loose. In know that these feelings affect my play. So when I'm "short," I don't try for long cross-court shots or down-the-line shots until I calm down. If I'm not calm, I will be hitting these shots too long. When I'm "long," I know I can hit*

> *more difficult shots with accuracy. I'll start out playing very ag-*
> *gressively when I feel "long" because I know I'm in good control*
> *of myself and my game.*
>
> *You can also walk to where you want your ball to land, or pace*
> *off the distance to a target you want to hit. The key here is to use*
> *the playing field, course, court, or track in another way to see*
> *how it changes as your tension level changes. This is a great way*
> *to prepare yourself for the game, and during the game.*

Your ritual is part of your personal power. Being powerful is knowing what you can do and when; and what you can't do and when. Learn as much from it as you can and apply it in all aspects of your life. Be your own experimenter and teacher.

We have moments in our lives in which everything is understood and we can do no wrong; unfortunately, these seem to be more than compensated for by moments in which even inanimate objects seem out to do us in. In these moments, all rituals are lost because the preparation was not complete or wrong.

> *You've dressed for a party*
> *And are going downstairs, with everything about you*
> *Arranged to support you in the role you have chosen,*
> *Then sometimes, when you come to the bottom step,*
> *There is one step more than your feet expected.*
> *And you come down with a jolt. Just for a moment*
> *You have the experience of being an object*
> *at the mercy of a malevolent staircase.*
>
> *[T.S. Eliot, "The Cocktail Party", 1950; quoted in Alan Watts,*
> Psychotherapy East and West, *1973, p. 96.]*

There are times when we get caught up in the uniquely perceived rituals of others. For example, a good friend of mine, who coaches a university football team, told me about a problem he was having with one of his defensive backs. This particular player, who was mediocre at best, accused the coach of never having liked him, and consequently not giving him enough playing time. Asked to explain his feelings, the player said, "Everyone knows that the farther away from the dressing-room door your locker is, the more likely it is that the coach doesn't like you." Since his locker was farther away than the other backs' lockers, he had concluded that he was the least liked. Although the coach demonstrated that there was no connection between locker location and his feelings toward the players, the unhappy young man held fast to tradition. Being a superb coach, my friend moved the player's locker into the hallway just outside the dressing-room — thus rendering it closest to the door.

It is impossible to describe your preparation in purely mechanical terms; its inner mechanisms are invisible from the outside. If we try to dismantle it, to get a closer look at its mechanics, it begins to stall and its wave-like motion stops, leaving nothing to see. We can see the ritual that contains your motions, but not how you conceive of the right questions and then go about answering them. We can see you pacing around the room, putting a golf ball in your office, and the cups of coffee and chewed-up pencils that you use to initiate and maintain your preparation, but no more.

The right preparation focuses your attention in a particular way so that you can become aware of the variety of implications and possible developments of your ideas. Here is an exercise to help you make the right preparation:

EXERCISE 2:4 *Take a deep breath. Before you exhale, one idea, one thought, one decision will come forward and strengthen as you exhale. Center your attention on it. Let everything else go on its own way. Make this experience of being calm a familiar one. As you do, you will sense that you have prepared yourself naturally and effectively.*

THE WRONG PREPARATION — *From Excitement to Anxiety*

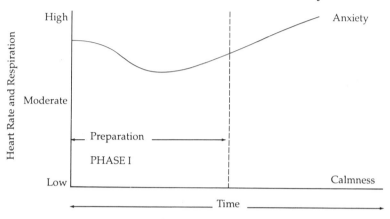

Wrong and right preparation both begin in excitement with some nervousness. While right preparation ends in calmness, wrong preparation concludes in rising anxiety. There is no "drop" to experience here. Instead, there is a rise in heart rate, irregular breathing, feelings of being rushed — and, of course, tension and stress. Any chance you had of calming down has come and gone. In fact, you didn't even give yourself the opportunity to be calm. You acted when you knew you weren't ready. You let indecision and doubt guide you, and they took full advantage of the situation. This leaves you with even more tension and feelings of being rushed because you have to make up for a poor effort and result. Making up for mistakes like this isn't an easy thing to do, as most of us already know. Once anxiety and indecision gain a foothold, they aren't about to leave without a good fight. The energy you'll need to win this struggle only takes you farther away from your intended goal, and can ultimately lead to feelings of exhaustion. The best strategy is not to get into this situation in the first place. This means creating as little turbulence for yourself as possible (see "Strategic Non-Interference, " Chapter 3). Not only is this an unusually effective strategy, it is one you can easily manage and use over and over.

The following exercises were designed to give you some ideas about how you can use the right strategy to overcome the wrong preparation, along with experience in actually doing it. Try each one to see how they feel and work, then work a strategy out for yourself and test it out.

STRATEGIES AND SOLUTIONS

Stepping Away   You cannot properly hit, throw, or kick a ball to a target with any accuracy if you are indecisive and anxious. You cannot move properly if you feel this way. Everything you try to do will be hurried, jerky, and complicated. The results you produce will be inconsistent and generally poor.

Never hit, throw, kick, or move if you are not ready. Step away and start over.

EXERCISE 2:5   *Learning to step away and come back again builds trust and confidence. It doesn't matter what activities you use; the important thing is that you learn to trust your decisions and actions. Stepping away dissipates unnecessary tensions and anxieties, and transforms resistance to useful energy. One of the great differences between amateurs and professionals is learning to "step away." It is part of the ritual of success. (See "Riding the Rapids," in Chapter 3.)*

Make a Tension Check   Pitchers feel tension in their legs, arms, and back; kickers in their upper legs and lower back; golfers in their shoulders, hands, hips, and ankles. In general, tension raises the shoulders, which leads to a tendency to overthrow or place the ball, or to swing over the top of the ball. For one professional golfer I worked with, tension pulled his hands at address from his front leg back toward the center of his body. This threw his balance off and he found himself swinging over the ball instead of through it. He corrected it simply by checking his hand position. If his hands were not lined up with the crease in his front pant leg, he moved them into this position. The distance his hands moved back from this crease became his way of checking on his tension level.

The same line of tension raised the gloved hand of a professional ice-hockey goaltender above his knees, and he was beaten low on that side far too often. He learned to check his glove to be sure that it was not above his knees. This correction was made with closed eyes. It was felt, and it was right.

Tightness can cause pitchers to release the ball later; cause batters to swing over the ball; and cause tennis, squash, and racquetball strokes to be mistimed.

EXERCISE 2:6 *While you are preparing, whether at work or at play or at home, take a moment to see what tension is doing to your body and correct it.*

Whatever activity you choose, when you feel tense, close your eyes and experiment with a number of moves until you feel you've found the right one. You can do it in a few tries. Trust yourself. You can also use Exercises 2:3 and 3:2 as a tension check.

Challenge Yourself A problem that comes up time and time again in my work with professional and elite amateur athletes involves coping with the inevitable anxiety that creeps into their game. Many of these athletes cope in a way that should interest you — they consciously became less motivated to prepare. They rely on mechanics, raw talent, even divine intervention to get them through. They disengage themselves from what they have to do, so that they can act without being responsible. It shows; their performance suffers the more they disengage. They do things half-way — or less.

This is a terrible strategy because not only does it not work, it creates more anxiety and frustration. In golf, this leads to what is called "the yips."

You cannot ride between the crests of the wave if you are thinking about how to stay afloat. In the same way, you

LACK OF MOTIVATION DURING PREPARATION

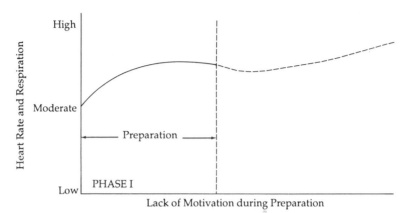

Lack of Motivation during Preparation

cannot speak if you are preoccupied with the rules of grammar. You have to let go, and trust yourself, to ride and speak.

One dark night a man was passing a dry well when he heard a cry for help from below. "What's the problem?" he called down.

"I am a grammarian, and I have unfortunately fallen, due to my ignorance of the path, into this deep well, in which I am now all but immobilized," responded the other.

"Hold tight. I've got to go get a ladder and rope," said the man.

"One moment, please!" said the grammarian. "Your grammar and diction are faulty; be good enough to amend them."

"If that's all that matters to you," shouted the man, "you'd better stay there until I can speak right."

And he went his way.

    [adapted from Idries Shah, Tales of the Dervishes, 1973, p. 193.]

There is a strong belief in North American and Europe that we exist as an ego, a self that inhabits a physical shell, apart from the outside world. Such a separation means that our minds are given the job of controlling our bodies. As a result, one part of ourselves is made responsible for controlling the other. In turn, this produces feelings that we consist of fragments of emotions, abilities, talents, and behaviors that are somehow attached to a central core — which we catch only rare glimpses of. Due to our own sense of being in bits and pieces, we divide the outside world in its turn into a series of separate events. To many of us, this seems a natural state of affairs.

It is not natural to be broken into separate pieces. It is not natural to be disturbed by changes in the world around us that, by and large, we have created for ourselves.

How can a person be taught to judge distance accurately for what he/she has to do — i.e., throw a ball, hit a target, reach a certain point in a race, attain a goal? The brain houses receptors of these distances; therefore such judgments cannot be taught from a purely mechanical framework. Judgments of distance must be learned. It must be felt, integrated, and used properly — but it has to be felt before it can be used.

In order to understand what "distance" is, we must be able to extend ourselves beyond ordinary boundaries. We release the mind to fly before us, obtaining information from sources remote from our physical location. This experience allows distance to be perceived and then coordinated with physical action. The goal is not as far away as we once thought.

EXERCISE 2:7 *Close your eyes and: walk around your house; walk to where you think your ball landed on a field after you have thrown or hit it; shoot baskets; swim; or run. Is this the same distance as when you performed these actions with your eyes open? Does the distance seem to be more fluid, expansive, or collapsible? Does distance change? Of course it does. Distance is not as absolute as mechanical methods teach us, but is instead related to our personal experiences. Learn what your distances are. Learn where your actions have an impact.*

The strategy needed here is one that will re-establish the natural rhythm of preparation: excitement to calmness. To do this, you must create a challenge for yourself that will excite you. Athletes might select a target that they can't be indifferent to: instead of landing a ball on a wide fairway, on the right side, they can pick a specific area and focus in on it.

If you are throwing to a target, make the landing area smaller and smaller. No matter what activity you use, set yourself a target that is tougher than you are used to. When you can hit it, make it even smaller.

Take Advantage of Mechanics: The Art of Hustling One of the easiest hustles in sport involves asking your opponent, "How did you make such a wonderful shot?" Ask why they held their arms a certain way, or why their elbow was bent, or how they set up for a shot. Once you get your opponents to focus on mechanics, even if they are technically better than you are, they will soon forget how to play. You will have broken their rhythm by planting seeds of doubt, and these seeds will flourish if your opponent takes your misdirected advice. Focusing on mechanics without intuition leads to mistrust. On the other hand, when mechanics are joined with intuition, trust is enhanced.

EXERCISE 2:8 *Challenge someone to a game who has just finished a lesson with a teaching pro. You can almost guarantee that their game will deteriorate as they try to incorporate the techniques they have just been taught. They won't be able to trust either their mechanics or intuition. But don't try this after they've learned this lesson.*

A Good Beginning Ensures a Good End The reliance on mechanics alone also creates problems in business. Organizations are constantly searching for, selecting, and training people to ensure their continued growth. Down the line, organizations may also be faced with the problem of employees who seem to have reached a plateau and remained there, and of employees who have performed well in the past but no longer do so. The ways in which they try to cope with hiring and firing overlook one important and essential detail: selecting and terminating systems tend to treat people as discrete units to be molded to, or separated from, an organization. But successful organizations are not made up of discrete units, any more than athletes are made up of solely of mechanics. The most successful organizations recognize that they are composed of mutually interdependent people and departments.

Selection and training systems that recognize this interdependence are also more successful than traditional ones. For example, suppose that a company needs to replace members of its sales force. If the recruiters use a traditional approach, they are really saying to themselves, "We'll hire many to get the few we need." They forget that each new salesperson has an effect on the company. These effects are difficult to predict, because the selection system used has been developed for a number of sales companies, not for this one specifically. Each new salesperson selected creates a network of dependencies, which may or may not mix well.

A good salesperson increases production, shipping orders, phone calls, paperwork, and profit. This ripple effect creates a self-propelling positive atmosphere among a number of levels in the company. A poor salesperson's network may on the other hand, involve shifting priorities and paperwork to other, less productive, areas; and these networks may cancel each other. Imagine what can happen as more and more people are selected along traditional lines.

Traditional selection may improve the chances of getting one or two good people, but at hidden costs: the creation of negative dependencies, and having to deal with poorly performing salespeople. Organizations use this method primarily because they don't have the patience to wait for one or two good people, and tend to forget what the hidden costs are.

It is far better to hire one good person than to hire many, hoping that one person is in there somewhere. Mistakes made at the beginning become more difficult to correct as time passes: just ask organizations that are "middle-heavy" with recruiting mistakes. *Select for interdependence, not for separateness, and your mistakes will be greatly reduced.* This guideline applies to your work, family, and social life.

3 *In the Trough of the Waves*

Riding in the Trough of the Waves

THE STAGES OF preparation and action are both joined and separated by a valley of timeless intensity that I have called the *trough of the waves*. The peaks or crests are the trough's borders. At its center is your Still Point (S.P.), your moment of greatest peace and strength. It is experienced not as a brief interlude but as an expansion of time, beyond the time in the world around you. Yet no matter how long you remain at the S.P., when you re-enter the world, only the briefest portion of measured time has passed.

The S.P. is a turning point — a finely adjusted balance of inner and outer time that transforms preparation into guided and effective actions. At the S.P., preparation and action are fused, then projected on a path that is natural, successful, and flowing. Actions guided by the decision you make at your S.P. (see Chapter 4) reflect your integrity and insight, and are felt to be benevolent and compassionate.

With practice and patience, you will come to know these landmarks very well. You will know them intellectually, emotionally, physically, intuitively. You will know just how far inside or outside the trough you are, and when you are at its very center. Here you are silent and still while letting everything pass before you. Here you can decide what is right and then do it.

THE CENTER OF THE STILL POINT: *The time and place of your greatest strength and tranquility*

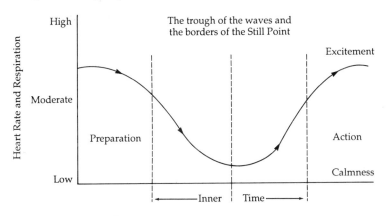

EXERCISE 3:1 *The regulation of breathing often helps to establish the boundary between Preparation and Stillness. The next time you are at a golf tournament, tennis or squash match, or basketball or baseball game, watch the players in a different way. Pay attention to how they are breathing as they set up for a shot, hit a serve, shoot a free throw, or make a pitch. Are they holding their breath, letting it out fast, or letting it out slowly? This will give you a good idea how they are controlling their anxiety. If they are holding their breath, it is a good bet they are anxious. If their breath is regular and slow, they are in very good control of themselves. Rapid and loud exhaling in competitive situations tends to signal fatigue, especially in boxing; it is also a sign of how an athlete is dealing with high levels of anxiety. The more rapid and loud the exhaling, the higher the anxiety.*

Now you can pay attention to your own breathing pattern in decision-making and action situations. The quieter your breathing, the slower you feel, the less turbulence there will be between you and your goals. Whatever turbulence is there is a reflection of yourself. Being prepared means you have begun the process of letting your thinking do your thinking. It means you have stopped getting in your own way. Any unnecessary anxiety will be absent, and you can experience a state of calm freedom to decide and act.

A Third Way

M ANY OF US were taught two basic ways to deal with the outside world: (1) to close down our senses and cut off the outside world; or (2) open ourselves wide and be lost in the outside world.

The first way removes the meaning from your life and from any actions you take. The second way ensnares you in a net that you cannot cut through.

What we were not taught is that there is a *third way*: to use your natural strength, your Rhythm, to bring together the inner and outer in a continual exchange. And this means riding in the trough of the waves of your Rhythm.

The *third way* cultivates your instincts, intuition, and intellect. Riding in the trough teaches you how to navigate in the deep stillness of your inner seas, and then how to cultivate your experience and turn it into motions that shape the events in your world. Navigating and cultivating require no special knowledge. They do require that you be silent and learn to listen to your inner voice, which speaks in a language that is perfectly and precisely understandable. Each word, sentence, and thought is exquisitely clear, as if each were made of the finest crystal.

The trough of the cycle, whose lowest point is the center of your S.P., can be thought of as the string of a bow that is stretched to its fullest, and at that point, is released. The arrow it sends toward your target is the guided and focused energy you have transformed into action.

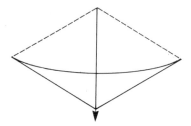

There is a pattern to every success and to every failure. *Reaching your S.P. is an essential feature of every successful action; in every failure, the S.P. has been avoided or forgotten.* The

Rhythm of a life of personal achievement and happiness has to contain an S.P. It is the foundation without which actions could not blend success with compassion.

To be still, focused, in control of yourself, and decisive is to be yourself. We tend to call these conditions altered states of consciousness, when they are instead the most natural of conditions. Not only is this a natural state, it is powerful and protective as well.

Understanding and living your life in accordance with a rhythmic pattern of perceptions and feelings means moving beyond purely intellectual thinking. By combining intuition and intellect, you can feel and see the interdependence between you and others, as well as that between the events in your world. Such a life is rich and takes you where the ordinary eye does not see. This is why many exercises in this book must be done with your everyday eyes closed.

A gentleman in his late fifties, recently recovered from cancer, came to one of our golf programs with the goal of driving a ball as far as he did before his cancer. He was about 30 or 40 pounds below his normal body weight, and felt weak. With his eyes open, he sprayed his drives all over the practice range, while complaining about the wind, the temperature, the balls, the noise. After some convincing, he agreed to try closing his eyes. Almost immediately his drives became long and straight, and he stopped complaining. Within a few days, his everyday eyes could see as well as his closed eyes, and he was gradually adding distance and accuracy to his drives and long irons.

Your normal waking consciousness is only one special type of awareness. Another is experienced at your S.P., when you look inside to see what is going on around you. Your thinking mind is silenced and shifts into an awareness that suspends and expands your personal time. Now you are in a postion to concentrate and decide. You have placed yourself in a state of meditative awareness and action at the same time. We have all achieved this state at one time or another, in play. And in play, the opportunity to repeat this moment over and over again is always there, waiting for you to discover it. In this moment, our senses and beliefs are totally absorbed in one movement, whether it is hitting a perfect 3-iron, throwing a dart, or running to a finish line. Insight, delight, and joy accompany such performance, as at other "sweet spots" in our lives.

At the S.P. there is no separation between you and time, or between what you want to produce and the actual results. Nothing can exist independently at the S.P. Here you begin to shape the events to come.

EXERCISE 3:2 *Select your target, but do not bring back your club or racquet, release a ball or dart, begin to run; write that letter you have been putting off, read a book you had started a week ago; or tackle any of those things around the house or at work that you really hate to do, until you are as quiet and still as you can be. Be patient and wait for the feeling of being solid and centered to come over you. Then, feel when you can let go and move. Do not imagine or fantasize, just turn your attention inward until you feel yourself turning outward again. At the turn, the centre of your S.P., your decisions and preparations will become actions, if you let it happen and trust yourself.*

Extraordinary Meaning: The Silence of Stillness

THE STILLNESS that exists in "the trough" is not ordinary stillness. It is not just being tranquil and calm, or being inactive and not hearing a sound. This form of stillness provides the freedom to experience all of that, and to feel the absence of unnecessary stress and tension. This leads to a feeling and perception that all things are interconnected, flowing into and out from each other in a series of defined patterns. In this stillness, no before or after exists, only the now from which you can see and decide your course of action. Your stillness lets you see the continuous dance of events parading by. This is "true" time — unpassing, personal time. The world outside is in another time, and as you remain quiet and still, you can see this other time pass by your eyes. You can easily jump into it whenever you want. Your decision to return will be based upon the results you want to produce.

In your stillness, which to you may seem like minutes but to your watch is only seconds, an extraordinary perception begins to grow. As your inner awareness merges with the outside, as you come to appreciate this fusion, you will learn that as you manage yourself, you are also influencing the events that pass by. As the distinction between the inner and the outer fades, so will the separation between your preparation, decisions, and actions. In this natural state of concentrated awareness, of understanding and compassion, you have flowed into the world by trusting yourself to remain tranquil and focused. No language can adequately describe this experience; perhaps the best characterization is "a feeling that what was once complicated is now simple and enjoyable." You will also have the feeling of being in possession of a powerful secret.

Your Still Point

A T YOUR S.P., all the things that you see and experience, all the actions you decide on, include you. You are the essential part of the process. You cannot be an independent observer anymore. Everything becomes part of your attitude, your beliefs, your ability to manage yourself. The world around you can only be understood in terms of dynamic and harmonious processes. You give this dynamic its texture and harmonies.

Three experiences are impossible at your S.P:

(1) you cannot have a "head cold" — that is, there are no dream-like or foggy perceptions;

(2) incomplete understanding is impossible because you are aware of yourself, the world around you, and the bond between the two at the same moment;

(3) you will not be able to reduce things to their smallest part — nor, for that matter, will you need to, because the

whole of what you want to do seems so simple that it resists being reduced any further.

Breaking things down into smaller and smaller fragments, then trying to piece them back together again, represents the basic premise of traditional mechanical approaches to teaching. This emphasis on reductionism has spawned a new generation of machines and expensive toys to examine movements from one microsecond to the next — for example, computer simulation of what ideal movements should be; video techniques that capture every flinch and blink in super-slow motion; wrist-watches that tell you how well you are performing compared to a great athlete.

These mechanically oriented approaches actually do accomplish a few goals, but not the ones they intended to: seeing people as machines, as these approaches do, is not only wrong (because it breaks them down into independent components), but is doesn't work. In spite of the marvels of technology, there have been no major improvements in performance — largely because these technical aids tend to disrupt the natural integrity and harmony of thought and action. These approaches are effective at breaking processes down, but much less so, when it comes to teaching people how to put them back together to produce fluid and simple actions. Mechanics alone cannot produce effective human actions.

You must forget about reducing, and instead feel how simple it is to let your actions flow from your moment of being still. When all the complexities are repressed, you become free to decide and do. The simplicity of this experience is most often felt by its "completeness," not by its parts. There are no breaks or changes of tempo. Combining mechanics with your Rhythm ensures simplicity, and the absolute feeling that what you did was correct and complete. Your Rhythm provides the tracks to keep your mechanics moving in the right direction without your having to think about it. Now you can enjoy and savour what you are doing. By joining mechanics with your Rhythm, you have achieved a natural unity of thought and action. This, in turn, changes what was once complex into what is now simple. Because everything is simple and understood, it seems perfectly natural — and what is natural is also successful. So now, that great shot you made will seem very simple; it can be realized again, and even surpassed.

Reaching Your Still Point

EXPERIENCING YOUR body provides a key to an understanding of the events around you. When you are healthy, you probably feel no separateness between the parts of your body. Instead, you experience your body as an integrated whole that produces a feeling of contentment and well-being. Feelings of being fragmented occur when you are ill; this produces separateness and, more often than not, feelings of being unable to control these different parts.

In our search for an understanding of reality, we have put our trust in science. We haven't paid much attention to the fact that science has recently re-discovered some ancient truths. Science seems to be homing in on one specific truth:

THE ULTIMATE REALITY IS THE REALITY WITHIN.

You have been there already. You have experienced the effortless flow of thoughts into action. There have been times in your life when your mind has become a source of invisible energy capable of setting into motion your visible behavior just as, for instance, invisible vibrations in the air set into motion the activities of your television. At such times, mind and body are training together, vibrating in harmonious cycles with one another. You have tended to think of these exhilarating moments as gifts that come and go on their own — but you are very much in control of their comings and goings. Fortunately, the methods for achieving control are simple, though challenging.

Subtle Power: Learning to Let go

ONE TYPE OF control involves the use of "Subtle Power." The first experience of Subtle Power occurs when you leave the excitement of preparation and enter the quietness of the next phase in your Rhythm.

THE FIRST BOUNDARY OF SUBTLE POWER

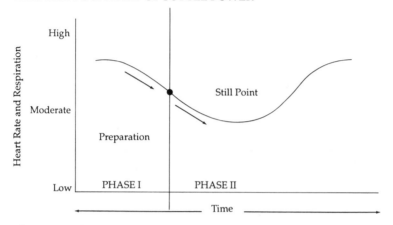

The second experience involves the feeling of change from being still to being active — the moment of "letting go." In order to ride into or out of the trough at the right speed, you have to let yourself go; you cannot force it in any way. At the same moment, you are in complete control.

THE SECOND BOUNDARY OF SUBTLE POWER

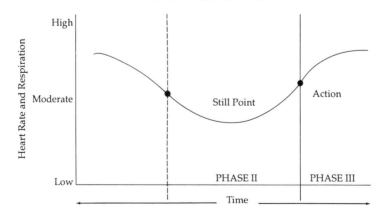

Subtle Power contains this paradox — you let go and are in control simultaneously. In this, it resembles that other seemingly contradictory state, at your S.P., where you are both tranquil and powerful. Any distinctions between letting to and being in control, and being tranquil and strong, are artifical and rapidly fade as you enter and leave the trough. These states exist in a natural balance that you become aware of as you experience the flow of your Rhythm. At first it comes unexpectedly; later you accept it as the way things should be.

Your heart rate may change by only 5 to 8 beats per minute, but you will feel the change. By letting go, you can feel the subtle forces between your mind and body. Letting go involves trusting yourself to be guided by your decisions. Trust allows tranquility to become energy, which completes the balance of the cycle of your Rhythm. Letting go also means that you are now completely free to move on to the next task.

When you experience Subtle Power, you cease to be anxious, aggressive, or manipulative. Instead, your decisions and actions shape events in more positive ways. Your life becomes free of noise, unnecessary tensions, and feelings of deep frustration. You stop creating trouble for yourself. Learning to let go accomplishes all of this because it clears the path for calmness and then action. With a clear view, you can get out of the way of any danger.

What do you need to let go of? To find out, turn to Appendix A and fill out the Job Stress Survey and Temper Scale.

The ride down from the crest of the first wave is accomplished by a feeling of effortless flowing. Part of this experience involves going beyond mechanics or techniques alone, while another part involves channelling your energies into doing without being distracted by your doubts. This is trust, not imitation. Trust the preparation and decisions you made, and you will be able to let go.

A good way to learn to let go and experience the moment to decide and act, is to learn to breathe properly. Breath is an immediate expression of the interplay between mind and body. The following exercises will give you the opportunity to practice "getting there." Please try them in the order presented.

EXERCISE 3:3   *This is a very important exercise: it helps you experience the lack of unnecessary tension in your body needed for making proper decisions.*

a. Take a deep breath, then let your breath out until it stops on its own. When you feel you have reached this point, ask a friend, spouse, or colleague to place one hand on your back and another on your chest, and push. If you have really let all your breath out, none will be left to rush out. At this point, your body will know what it is like to be without everyday tensions.

For many of us, air does rush out. How much is forced out is a good indication of the level of residual tension your body carries around every day. Tension interrupts the exchange of breaths, causing us to retain unnecessary and even harmful wastes. Panic breathing and short bursts of breath that do not bring relief may result when tension interferes with the natural in-and-out exchange of breaths. By contrast, proper breathing is the link between technique and outcome.

b. With your mouth slightly open, listen to the sound "HH" as you breathe in. When you can hear this sound, focus your thoughts. As you practice, your thoughts will become absolutely clear.

c. Put your fingers or a good pair of earplugs in your ears and pay attention to your inner sounds. When these are all you can hear, the thought that enters your consciousness is the correct one. Trust yourself.

d. Focus your attention on the pause between your in-breath and out-breath. During this pause, your thoughts will be both clear and correct.

EXERCISE 3:4

a. Take as deep a breath as you can, then float on your stomach across a swimming pool. Do not kick or use your arms. Let all your breath out gradually. Have a friend, spouse, or colleague place one hand on your back and the other on your chest, and push. The amount of air that rushes out is an index of the residual tensions you are carrying around. When little air rushes out, you will know what letting go feels like.

b. Hold on to the edge of the pool, and take a deep breath. Then, with your head underwater and legs and arms stretched out, expel your breath. Focus on doing it as slowly as possible. A feeling of timeless flowing will come over you as you control your breathing more and more.

The separation of thought and action is one of the limiting factors in the development of powers of concentration. Bringing thought and action together is the foundation of "unlimited powers" of concentration (see Chapter 5), intuition, and strength. This new power flows into your body and mind, and is directed outside only to return again. Success is assured because there is no feeling of being in pieces and separate from yourself and your actions. This is the experience of being still and in control. Your decisions are correct and you will feel and know it! New power comes into being as the mind learns to train the body and the body trains the mind.

There are a lot of people who cannot stand the tension of waiting.

These are the ones who have two alternatives: either to stand the tension of waiting or to be harmed by it.

> [Idries Shah, Reflections, 1972, p. 126]

I can't leave my mind on the [diving] board. I have to stay in the present. I have to be relaxed enough to clue into my

*memory tape of how to do it . . . not just to do it right, but
to do it right from all the wrong places.*
> [*Champion diver Greg Louganis, quoted in Joe Flower,
> "Secrets of the Masters," 1987, p. 129]*

The process of learning about yourself is real. It is based on
your experience and feelings, which are certainly real. In-
itiating the process involves turning your perceptions inward, away from the shadows of the world, away from
their traditional hold over you. You need a new mirror to
the world — one that you look into with your eyes closed.
With eyes closed, the reaching-out tendencies of the conscious mind are stilled as your attention is turned inward.
The outer world vanishes, as does the "I" that has preven-
ted you from achieving your goals. Within this stillness,
you can experience the self; such an experience reveals a
truth that leads into proper action.

*What I must do is all that concerns me; not what the people
think. . . . It is easy in the world to live after the world's
opinion; it is easy in solitude to live after our own; but the
great man is he who is in the midst of the crowd keeps with
perfect sweetness the independence of solitude.*
> [*Ralph Waldo Emerson, quoted in Juan Mascaró,* Lamps of Fire,
> *1972, p. 83]*

Return, now, having experienced the power of letting go,
to another exercise in trust.

EXERCISE 3:5 *Select an activity — throwing a ball to a target
or to a person, jumping, swimming, or just walking around your
home or office — and perform it with your eyes closed. This is an
exercise in trust and feeling the results develop without seeing in
the usual way. Keep trying until you can reach your target or
not bump into anything.*

Riding the Rapids

A S YOU MOVE through the trough of the waves toward its center and beyond, you may experience a rougher ride than you expected. This usually happens soon after your first trip through, because your old conscious attitudes are fighting for survival. They are resisting the intrusion of new ways of doing things, and trying to re-establish themselves. Although this has all the makings of quite a conflict, don't be overly concerned about it — just come up with a game plan. One plan that works remarkably well also turns out to be easy and even familiar. You tried this exercise earlier: just step away and start again.

EXERCISE 3:6 *How many times have you stood over a golf ball, or set up to hit a target, whether it be a bullseye, a basketball net, home plate, or a nine-ball, and felt you just couldn't do it? Perhaps some minor distraction became the focus of your complete attention and you lost that feeling of confidence; or some voice caused feelings of anxiety, a certainty that what you were trying to do wouldn't work. And how many times have you gone ahead and tried to do it anyway? The results of acting when you've lost your focus often turn out far different than you wanted, leaving you to make up for a poor outcome. Instead, simply step away and try it again.*

Whenever you stand over your golf ball, or prepare to make a free throw or to serve a tennis or squash ball, and you don't feel right for any reason, stop and start over again—yes all over again, from shot selection to getting ready to make the shot. Remember: first prepare by letting your excitement work for you (Phase 1); then allow yourself to be quiet and still (Phase 2); now let go and make the shot (Phase 3). It is in Phase 2 that you must learn to step away. So first practice putting, throwing a basketball, or hitting your serves by going through all three stages. When you have done that, recall events or things people that cause anxiety after you have completed Phase 1. Feel the difference between this condition and when you are still and quiet.

Now complete your shot. Feel what happens: how is this experience different from a shot that flows out of your S.P.?

Now do it again, but step away in Phase 2 and go back to Phase 1. Prepare, decide, and execute all over again. With practice, you can get back to your S.P. and perform effectively. You might be thinking as you read this that it will take too long to go back to Phase 1 again. Time it and see. Golfers learning to step away at first guess that it will take 20 to 30 seconds to do it again. Yet they typically average about 4 to 9 seconds. Wouldn't you rather take the time to step away and avoid the frustrations of lost shots, and the additional time needed to recover?

The "Sweet Spot": From Stillness into Action

THE S.P. IS a natural link joining preparation and doing. Traditional ideas about how these two are connected have been based on a straight-line model.

THE TRADITIONAL MODEL: *Preparation — Action*

Straight-Line Prediction

The Present ——————————————————The Future

This description has tended to work, within limits, with laboratory rats running mazes in search of food while avoiding electrically charged floors and doors that won't open, and with pigeons pecking away at colored dots on panels. Regrettably, the straight-line model hasn't worked well at all for people, because it fails to account for their unique abilities and temperaments. On the other hand, a model based on the Rhythm's cycle combines a person's strengths and desires so that appropriate action emerges out of preparation and decision-making. This model bends the straight line to form a flowing, wave-like motion, describing a person's Rhythm.

THE RHYTHM MODEL:

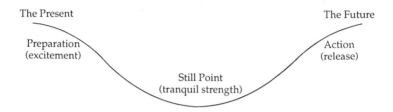

The straight-line model is an out dated illusion. The Rhythm, on the other hand, is not merely a descriptive model; it is the experience itself of preparing, deciding and acting successfully, without apparent effort. At your S.P., you open a door to let yourself be guided without creating any resistance to your actions. Leaving your S.P. is a natural part of your rhythmic pattern of personal understanding and success.

Within the S.P. you are in synch with a pulse that is protected from time and place. Your movements are flowing, unhurried. You can attend to all those details that need to be dealt with rather than being engulfed by them. The pulse of your thoughts and actions will not allow anything to go wrong; no distractions can cross your mind. Very simply, you act in an intuitive, self-directed, and natural way.

You cannot feel like a passenger in your own body, with some of its parts under your direction while others are listening to a voice you do not hear. Since your actions and thoughts are flowing from your experience at the S.P., they are complete, as you are, and express the integrity of your beliefs. Beyond the S.P. is the time of doing and of cultivating. Your powers have become real. Here you can experience how your understanding of your inner self is transformed into active participation in the outside world.

This is what is meant by integration of mind and body. This is a "peak experience" in which you have maximized your abilities and intellect. It is a "sweet spot" in your life, for you are at the right time and place, and in the right frame of mind. Acting on your hunches or being known as a clutch hitter become easy when you learn to leave your S.P., and *attend to* and *not be engulfed by* the circumstances around you.

The primary accomplishments of reaching and leaving the S.P. are to cultivate the inner mind, stabilize yourself so you can foresee and influence, and leave things better than when you found them. Exposure to the S.P. naturally untangles the knots in your life, and smooths out its fabric. This gives you the opportunity to test your new understanding, to cultivate strengths and discard weaknesses, and to release the weight of doubts and anxieties that have held you back.

A professional golfer I worked with provided a clear and practical example of being at the Still Point, and being outside its boundaries. When he became tense and anxious, he became "speedy." His motion from backswing to follow-through was an unbalanced blur. In this state, he took fewer than 19 seconds to select a club, address the ball, and strike it. The results were unpredictable, even to him. When he was calm, he took between 26 to 28 seconds to accomplish the same set of actions, with predictably good results. The center of his Still Point was between 12 and 14 seconds. He became a good judge of the right time to bring his club back, and so did his caddy. Once he told me, after a good round, that he felt so slow he had to check his watch — yet it turned out that this "exceptionally slow" round was 5 minutes and 40 seconds faster (with 3 fewer strokes) than his average. As being slow became more natural, he began to notice how faster other, less successful, players moved.

Return to the exercises on breathing (3:3) and try them again.

Strategic Non-Interference: How Not to Create Turbulence

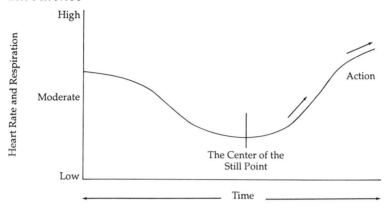

As you move from your S.P. into action, you will want to create as little turbulence as possible. You don't want to battle against any old or new barriers. You just need to release your energies into action. By retaining the inner calmness you achieved during the S.P., you will be able to resist any temptation to force or manipulate. Instead of having to ward off such distractions, which take so much of your useful energies, you will develop an instinct to act when situations are at their simplest, when your actions will have the most impact.

Actions guided by calmness are never *reactive*. Reactions create resistance to further actions. Not only are activities that flow from the S.P. non-reactive, they are creative and complete. To an outside observer, your immediate actions do not, in any way, interfere with events or people, yet their impact is clear and direct. This is *strategic non-interference*: a method of dealing with problems not by controlling what can be managed, but by conceiving, shaping, and bringing to fruition the decisions made at the S.P. Strategic non-interference *never underestimates the resistance you, yourself, can create*. This method also ensures that leaving the S.P. is accomplished without having to fight against the current in the trough of the waves. Using this method you can work your way around any resistance, and ultimately wear it away.

*During the reign of the legendary Emperor Yao, from 2357
to 2205 BC, China was plagued by devasting seasonal
floods. Emperor Yao enlisted Yu's father to oversee the control of China's rivers by building a series of dikes. He failed
after nine years of effort. The next Emperor, Shun, asked Yu
to complete his father's work, and Yu took on the project,
but with a different approach. Instead of trying to fight the
rivers, he had them dredged and channelled so they could
more easily reach their goal, the sea, thereby bringing the
floods under control.*

[C.L. Wing, The Tao of Power, 1986, p. 63]

Because you have limited the turbulence in front of you,
there is really no need to defend your beliefs, or deal with
feelings of resentment and fear. Since you did not react, but
let your actions radiate, what you do will seem natural and
correct. Strategic non-interference represents a state of intellectual independence consisting of both personal
knowledge and vision, and the confidence to apply them.
This is personal power.

In contrast, compulsive, neurotic, non-productive actions arise out of a separation of knowledge and vision and
trust. This sort of interference achieves dependence. It is
impossible under such conditions to be alert and attentive
because so much of your energy is consumed by non-
productive, self-protective rituals. Neurotic behavior follows a pattern that has its own peculiar path, which goes
in an opposite direction from that of your Rhythm, and
creates a turbulent barrier to action.

The executive, manager, or athlete who was once
productive and is now stagnant has created a turbulence
barrier that has held him/her in one place. The kind of re-
training that needs to be done in these situations is not job-
training, but self-training. Without understanding the self
first, no training can be successful.

Non-interference strategies are free of unnecessary agita-
tion or commotion, and of noise. They are tuned to the
sound of the harmonies between mind and body, a sound
that cannot be heard outside the S.P. This is the sound of

STRATEGIC NON-INTERFERENCE

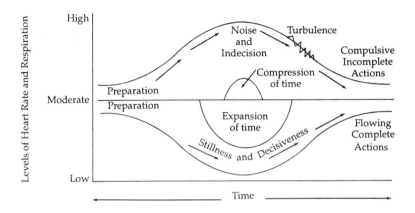

health, productivity and joy — a sound that overcomes turbulence and promotes healing. Let me give an example of how this sound can be used as a guide to the healing process.

To give me an idea of how my body was reacting to a long bout of low-back pain, my chiropractor hooked me up to a sounding device and let me hear my body through an amplifier. When he ran a small transmitting bar over an area of pain, I heard static. This was the sound of resistance, of the fight between my nerves, muscles, and mind. As I improved, the static turned to a series of clear harmonic tones. I could actually hear my body getting well while, at the same time I could feel it getting better. I realized what a wonderful sound this was about three weeks later, when I heard radio and television programs replaying the sounds sent back by Voyager as it journeyed through the universe on its way toward the rings of Saturn. The sounds were indistinguishable from the simple harmonic tones of my body becoming healthy. I now know that when we listen to our inner selves, we are hearing the sounds of our universe. When we're healthy, the sounds match perfectly; and when we are ill, there is static.

One way you can get an idea of the pattern of change in your life is to fill out the Daily Rating Schedule in Appendix A.

Learn to work with the grains of your nature and not against it.

[R.L. Wing, The Tao of Power, 1986, p. 51]

4 The Right Time: From Decision-Making To Action

The Change from Stillness to Action

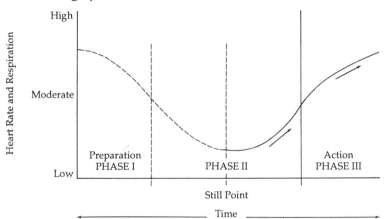

AT THE END of the first phase of your Rhythm, Preparation turns into a state of quiet decisiveness. At the center of this time of tranquility the process of transformation continues, to create a period of concentrated awareness. This awareness provides the groundwork for the next change — a time of anticipation and the readiness to act. These feelings signal that you are coming up out of the trough of the Still Point onto the crest of a wave of action. This is the final change in the complete cycle of your Rhythm. Your inner thoughts, ideas, images, and needs, having travelled through the Still Point, now become clearly directed action. The right action always flows from right preparation and stillness. It will feel absolutely right if you didn't try to manipulate it.

Feeling right follows from simply trusting yourself. When things are right, no turbulence arises between being still and being active. Turbulence makes any change from one phase of your Rhythm to another difficult, if not impossible. Instead of a smooth exchange of thoughts into action, turbulence produces compulsive and non-productive behavior. Futhermore, your pleasure in doing something you've wanted to do and are ready to do diminishes if you're worrying about or trying to defend what you are doing.

The change from being still to being ready to act is a turning point you must experience and feel. A rise in your heart rate and breathing tells you when to move out of the trough. You must actually feel this rise, no matter how small or large it is; some professional golfers can sense a change of from 3 to 5 heartbeats per minute. At first, the ride up to the crest of the wave can feel like moving through an uncharted seascape. Staying on the crest can be exhilarating and feel unsteady simultaneously. With practice, the ride will be so natural and feel so right and simple that you will wonder why you haven't taken this trip more often. Again, you must trust yourself to feel, and act on, the change. You must *let yourself go* to ride out of the trough and up on the crest. When you've done that, you will know that personal power comes from trusting yourself to act and letting things happen.

With practice, you will fine-tune the rising change; eventually, the right time will become so clear that all you have to do is act. You will experience this moment so strongly that it will become your personal trigger into action. For some of us, everything suddenly appears so clear that all doubt is gone. For others, everything seems to be in slow motion. You may experience this moment of change as part of an inner time sense, so that you know when the moment is coming and when it's gone.

In Game 5 of the NBA playoffs between the Boston Celtics and Detroit Pistons there was one play that neither team will forget; nor will their fans. Detroit's Isiah Thomas lobbed a soft pass to Bill Laimbeer, who was just a few feet away. Larry Bird of the Celtics anticipated the pass and rushed toward Laimbeer, supposedly intending to foul him, but he somehow managed to grab the pass. He kept his balance and turned toward the basket. Instinctively he knew there was a better shot to take than a low-percentage jumper. He spotted Dennis Johnson moving toward the basket. He made a great pass; Johnson made a difficult right-handed layup from the left side. The basket gave Boston a 108–107 win. Later, Bird said that Thomas' pass "seemed to hang up there forever."

[Jack McCallum, "The Mystique Goes On," *Sports Illustrated*, 1987, p. 32]

Decision-Making

To UNDERSTAND what you are trying to achieve, imagine the executive board of a major corporation sitting down to a meeting while onlookers drink beer, chomp peanuts or hot dogs, and can applaud or jeer at any moment. Boardrooms, offices, and living-rooms are not usually equipped with stands and concession booths or subject to the invasion of privacy insured by the presence of television cameras and commentators.

Let's extend this scenario a little further. In sports, officials, coaches, and athletes must not only make on-the-spot decisions, but also live with the immediacy of their impact. On the other hand, business executives and parents usually allow some time delay to see how their decisions actually work out.

People involved in sports can provide us with tremendous insights into how to make a decision, act on it, and handle reactions to it. Yet most research on decision-making has remained in the narrow confines of the lab and controlled experimentation, ignoring the playing field, the workplace, and the home. A coach making a decision on the bench late in a tight game, a quarterback calling an audible, a pitcher looking in to get a sign, an executive faced with a decision that will affect hundreds of employees, a parent trying to answer a child's questions about what it means to be critically ill — all have very little to do with a college sophomore faced with a battery of tests or a series of buttons to push, or a mouse trying to find its way out of a maze to reach a food dish.

Outside the controlled environment of the lab, different forces operate: to understand them is to uncover the profound dynamics of making decisions that work. For this reason I spent over 12 years studying people who have to make decisions and act on them in the public arena, whether they be novices or professionals. My work has shown, over and over again, the same practical and direct relationships between decision-making and performance.

These relationships can be best described in the form of three principles:

1. Do not ever take an action if you are indecisive;

2. It is far better to be decisive and be wrong than to act with indecision;

3. It is easier to make a recovery if your actions result from being decisive (even if you are wrong) than if your actions result from indecision.

These principles can be further distilled to one fundamental rule of effective decision-making:

BE DECISIVE.

In addition to these three principles and one fundamental rule, personal factors come into play in all decision-making. Excellent decision-makers share three things in common:

1. They are in control of themselves (e.g., they know how to reach their Still Point);

2. They have acquired sufficient knowledge in a given situation;

3. They have the ability to sense the flow of the situation.

In other words, the "style" of these decision-makers combines self-control and information with a sense of when to act. This style also describes a "clutch player," a leader, a person who has an "edge" — in short, a person who can be counted on to come through.

Indecision Will Get You Nowhere

ONE OF THE cardinal principles I have learned over the past decade of research is that any action based on indecision fails, reducing the effectiveness of later actions while leading to more indecision.

Recovery after being indecisive involves a long, hard battle against the self. If you have been indecisive, you don't know if your techniques are at fault, your thinking, a combination of both, or some unknown factor. For many people, recovery comes too late. How often has your game picked up after it's too late for you to win? Why do you play so much better after you have blown an opportunity to make a realistic comeback?

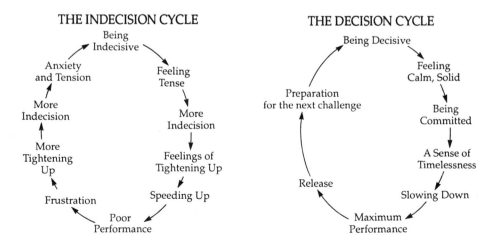

THE INDECISION CYCLE

Being Indecisive

Anxiety and Tension

Feeling Tense

More Indecision

More Indecision

More Tightening Up

Feelings of Tightening Up

Frustration

Speeding Up

Poor Performance

THE DECISION CYCLE

Being Decisive

Feeling Calm, Solid

Preparation for the next challenge

Being Committed

A Sense of Timelessness

Release

Slowing Down

Maximum Performance

Indecision breeds fatigue, tension, and frustrations, on the course, court, or field, at home or work. When you finally get to the point where tension has done all it could, you begin to play better.

Keep in mind that:

1. Involvement in what you are doing is characterized by being decisive; and

2. The signal that you are ready to act is your feeling of being quiet, secure, and solid. This feeling derives from the decrease in your heart rate accompanied by controlled breathing and a lack of muscular tension.

Professional golfers can take from 4 to 6 shots to recover from an indecisively executed shot. This happens because the golfer is trying to hit the next shot while still thinking about the last shot. Not even professional golfers, who play one of the greatest mind games of all, can be in two places at the same time.

Neither can baseball pitchers. Lacking in decisiveness and calmness, a pitcher produces a motion noted for its quickness and uncontrolled style. A pitcher now rationalizes, "If I am fast enough, my pitch will be powerful and accurate." However, unless proper mental preparations and physical actions accompany a timed and coordinated throw, an indecisive and inaccurate pitch results.

The same relationship between decisiveness and indecisiveness holds for all sports — indeed, for all situations that require making and acting on a decision.

Picture yourself as a figure skater going into a triple jump. You obviously can't stop and start over again if you're not ready. You must tune your routine to your Rhythm: be sure that you are relaxed going into your jump, release your tension during the jump, and are relaxed again upon landing. Your routine is an extension of your ability to control yourself. Be uncertain and your routine will be flawed.

WHAT BEING DECISIVE IS LIKE FOR PITCHERS

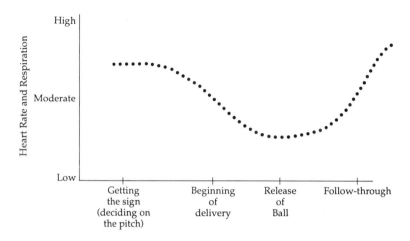

WHAT BEING INDECISIVE IS LIKE FOR PITCHERS

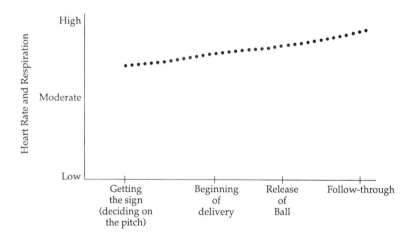

In everyone's life, a cycle of doubt occasionally creeps in. By tenaciously holding on to biases and old ways of thinking, you can lose what you want to gain — self-control. This is the paradox of decision-making.

Once you have the necessary knowledge, let go, let the moment be right for you. Rather than being indecisive, you will have achieved a moment of unwavering, unmoving wisdom.

Decision-Making and Being Right

E FFECTIVE decision-making comes when you use your Rhythm. Being in Rhythm means seeing the interdependence of the pieces, then forming a whole that is the basis of your decision and action. Trusting your Rhythm to guide you, even if it takes you beyond an awareness that you are not familiar with, is a natural feature of decision-making. Your Rhythm is *not* a consultant. It should not be used to confirm what you already know but to discover what you need to know. It will help you to sense the interdependence, the opportunities, and the right moment to act.

All the events in our lives are created by and filtered through the mind. They arise from a particular, and oftentimes unique state of consciousness that dissolves and reappears in a pattern constituting an integral part of our daily routine. You create best in a relaxed state of consciousness. In this state, you turn inward; in this turning, you find the great incubator for making decisions — your true self. The more ambiguity your world contains, the greater the degree of uncertainty or risk, the more effective your calmness will be.

"Reasonable people always see things in the same way," said the Khan of Samarkand to Nasrudin one day.

"That is just the trouble with 'reasonable people'," said Nasrudin; *"they include at least some people who always see only one thing out of a potential of two possibilities."*

The Khan called his advisors to explain, but they thought Nasrudin was talking nonsense. The next day Nasrudin rode through town on a donkey in such a way that his face was towards the donkey's tail.

When he arrived at the palace where the Khan was sitting with his advisors, Nasrudin said: "Would your highness please ask the people what they have just seen?"

When asked, they all said: "A man riding back-to-front on a donkey."

"That is exactly my point," said Nasrudin. "The trouble with them all is that they did not notice that perhaps it was me who was right and the donkey the wrong way around."

[Idries Shah, Caravan of Dreams, 1972, pp. 30–31]

Whether you prefer to see coaches and officials as the Khan's advisors, as Nasrudin, or as the donkey, this parable points to some of the complexities and humor that encompasses the relationship between these two groups and players — not to mention the fans.

Psychologists and sociologists interested in the study of sports have ignored both officials and coaches in favor of the players. This represents a serious oversight, given the number of important games affected by their decisions.

Officials and coaches must anticipate and make very quick decisions in an emotionally charged and public environment while so-called "Big Business" has long recognized the need for discrete decison-making. This may be one trouble spot in the trend in today's management decision-making toward viewing office managers as coaches. The public scrutiny and pressures on coaches, from which most managers are well shielded, represent the key and deciding factor separating the two. Moreover, officials and coaches not only must make on-the-spot decisions but are accountable for the immediate, and public, impact of those decisions.

Whatever your views about officials and coaches, remember that few groups in our society make decisions under such pressured circumstances. We therefore have a good deal to learn from them. Over the years, my colleagues and I have had the opportunity to talk with and observe many officials and coaches. What we have learned, I would like to share with you now.

Three basic areas that have a direct influence on performance concern these groups.

1. **Control of the game is the job. This means walking the line between directing the game and being a disciplinarian.**

Officials and coaches seem to be caught up in an old and sticky trap that middle-managers and parents of teenagers know all too well. Playing the role of facilitator means giving the players flexibility, and running the risk that the limits of that flexibility could stretch out too far to pull back in. Managers who treat employees as individuals who are capable of working on their own with some direction (theory Y) run the risk of having a group of employees who do work well but not necessarily to achieve the goals of the organization.

When officials and coaches become diciplinarians, they become the focus of the game, and the flow of play suffers. Managers and parents sometimes decide to take this "path of least resistance": in doing so, they embrace another theory of management (theory X) according to which people are inherently lazy, lack any real motivation to work, and are only interested in rewards. Getting people to do any work requires close supervision and swift punishment.

Both these theories no doubt hold partially true for everyone. Successful officials and coaches, however, have learned to make use of a third theory: trying to control the game. They understand from experience that in order to control the game they must be perceived by players and other officials and coaches to be in control of themselves. This, then, is the key to all forms of management — control of yourself comes first.

2. You must know the rules and know how to apply them.

Now, this sounds simple enough — but players and other coaches can show a remarkable ignorance of these same rules. Imagine trying to explain to a team captain or coach why you have applied a rule in a certain way when they act as if you are speaking in a long-dead language. Imagine trying to explain a change in company policy to an employee who has been on the job for years, or explaining to your teenagers why you have grounded them for the weekend.

You cannot control the game unless you know the rules and how to interpret them under a variety of circumstances. If you get a reputation for knowing the rules better than others, you will have an edge. Knowing when to apply them will give you another.

A hockey coach I worked with for a number of years had a wonderful reputation around the league because he knew just how far a rule could be bent. For example, his team's bench was always higher than the visitors'. Opposing players had a tough time climbing over the boards just to get to the ice, and this eventually tired them out. He also had his team's bench extended almost the full length of the rink so that his players could get out on the ice to receive a pass or stay ahead of the rush of an opposing player. Needless to say, the rules were changed, but he still found others to get around.

Another coach would start a game one player short just to keep his team sharp. Sometimes it worked so well he played an entire game this way.

One of the most irrepressible, loved, and respected baseball managers, Bill Veeck, will always be remembered for his pinch-hitting midget. After all, if the strike zone extends from a player's knees up to his chest, why not make it harder for a pitcher by making the zone smaller? Because of Veeck, more and more players began to use a crouched rather than a more upright stance.

These coaches and managers controlled the game because the opposing team, and the fans, expected them to do something different. They controlled by using the anticipation of others.

3. **Although (1) and (2) certainly represent important factors, the most crucial concern is the ability to sense the flow of the game.**

When the game flows, officials, coaches, and managers become virtually invisible. Yet they are most in control during such games. This is one of the oldest models of leadership that has come to us from the Orient: *the best and wisest leader leads least.*

In North America, we have some problems with "leading least." It smacks of a totally laissez-faire attitude that we believe to be nice in theory but terrible in practice. Yet, as one official told me, "If knowledge of the rules, the ability to interpret them, decision-making ability, and remaining composed are applied properly, then *you have formed the flow of the game.*" When both game-control and self-control are present, everyone — either in the game, or watching it — feels the natural flow. Sensing the flow also means that an official's call or coach's decision is a product of concentration and anticipation. A correct call or decision cannot be made without both of these qualities working together, blending into each other.

Sometimes things go so well for one team that it seems like they have their opponents' playbook. Allie Sherman was coaching the New York Giants against the Cardinals. After the game, which the Giants won handily, Cardinal quarterback Charley Johnson told Sherman that every time he looked at the Giant's defensive sets, he knew Sherman had anticipated what play he had called.

Incorrect calls or decisions are invariably a result of either a lack of concentration or anticipation of an event that doesn't happen — for example, gearing your defense to a run on a crucial third down and two attempt, and watching your secondary gets beaten on a long pass.

Successful officials and coaches have learned how to concentrate, anticipate, and decide under unusual pressures. Whatever we can learn from them about how to cope with such stresses while remaining sensitive to the flow of the game can only help us deal with our own day-to-day stresses and crises. Aside from the three concerns officials and coaches have — control, knowledge and application of the rules, and sensing the flow — *rituals* help keep things together in sport, from spitting chewing tobacco at specific targets on dugout floors to placing pyramids under the team's bench as Red Kelly did when he coached the Toronto Maple Leafs.

Braincalming, Not Brainstorming

THE TERM "brainstorming" has become part of the stock language of decision-making — in particular, creative decision-making. Some associate it with retreats in either rugged or luxurious settings, and view it as a cornerstone of so-called "think tanks."

Let us suppose for a moment that there really is such a thing as a brainstorm. What is going on during the "storm"? Picture the brain — the seat of sensation, memory, imagination, intellect — subjected to a violent disturbance, buffeted by high winds, feeling the turbulence of the waves of each thought, troubled, unable to cope with a tumultous rush of images and ideas. This is a brainstorm! When we experience such sensations, no creative outcome is possible. Survival, not creativity, becomes our priority. Storms result in havoc and destruction, not positive change and growth.

You cannot feel relaxed while the storm is brewing. Thoughts jump in and out of awareness, following an erratic path that seems to be outside of your control. You feel these jumps and shifts in thoughts and feelings as tension and anxiety. These negative emotions, in turn, set up barricades to finding the routes that converge on the right solutions. The greater the intensity of the storm, the more rapid and frequent are the jumps, and the faster the barricades go up. All this movement set ups an illusion of excitement followed by real exhaustion. Your anxiety has taken over.

To be creative, to be decisive, the brain should be calm, quiet, without turbulent waves. A calm brain is powerful, capable of joining together what at first seems radically different or irrelevant. The power of calmness rests in its ability to integrate, not fragment.

A calm brain has the power to change the negative to the positive. To be calm is to be anchored and balanced — to judge, anticipate, and act because you are still and able to see the patterns of movements around you. In group decision-making, calmness interlocks each person, recognizing their independence and interdependence at the same time.

In a state of braincalming, your ability to integrate information is increased. You create new channels for eliminating and selecting information. You use your personal experience in a positive and beneficial way for yourself and others. You take down all the barricades and travel freely.

Braincalming occurs when you are in Rhythm. It is being at your Still Point, expanding it, and using your powers. It is taking the opportunity and time to wonder, and the freedom to look for the right answer. Answers can come as a sudden insight, and, when reached in this way, are very often accompanied by feelings of joy and amusement at having completed part of a wonderful journey and waiting to begin another.

The essential characteristic of productive decision-making and subsequent action then, is to be calm and strong.

Insight

EFFECTIVE decision-making also requires centering on your sensations about an idea, on its ties to other ideas, and on how it sets them into motion. The rippling movement of these ideas constitutes a vital ingredient of what we call "insight." Insight involves feeling both passive and active at the same time. You remain still and yet you are in action in what seems like the very same moment. In this timelessness, you experience no negativity or doubt. You feel only the experience of discovery.

Each of us has had the experience of insight, but few of us understand how it comes about, because insight seems to be so "sudden" and "accidental."

Your decision's presence has been felt but, until now, unseen. Only now does it become clear and vivid. Thus it appears sudden, as if it came "out of the blue." It did not come from the blue; nor was it sudden. It happened while you were at your Still Point. The more often you are able to reach this point and expand it, the less sudden or accidental insight will seem. You may need to find another word to label this experience.

The "sudden" appearance of your decision represents a personal insight. Without unnecessary barriers to get around, or anxiety to block your view, you are able in perfect calm to generate enormous powers. You did not have to waste any of your power to take the barriers down or figure out a way to get around them. As your reward for being calm, you achieve a clear and unobstructed view. This clarity of seeing makes your decision insightful.

The Right Time

AN ARCHER DRAWS the bow, focuses on this feeling, aims, and lets go. Anyone can draw a bowstring, but it takes an archer to know when to let go. For an archer, the drawing and letting go are in balance.

An important part of the decision-making process is timing. The right time is contained in the Still Point. The Rhythm of your golf swing (tennis stroke, free throw, running pace, or business or family decisions) contains a preparation and outcome joined by a moment that tells you to bring the club or racquet back, release the ball, let go, decide, and trust that you will be successful. The trigger for making your decision and acting on it occurs during the Still Point. It is a sense of being solid, grounded, balanced: a feeling of being emptied of all thoughts but one — that of being slow. It is never focused on results.

The Rhythm of the successful archer, golfer, pitcher, or other athlete is the same, and it runs through all decision-making situations. Learn to reach the Still Point and to ride in its trough, and you will observe what a powerful ally it can be.

EXERCISE 4:1 *You have been examining documents, reports, and memos full of advice for days. Now, the time has come to reach a decision. First, calm yourself with one of the breathing* *exercises from Chapter 3. Do not think about your decision while you're doing this. Pick up your putter and take some practice putts. Get into your Rhythm. When you feel you are putting in Rhythm, tell yourself that on the 7th putt (or whatever number has significance for you), you will decide. Use your Still Point on this putt to make the decision. You could also shoot baskets, run, walk, swim, serve a tennis or squash ball, shoot pucks, or just play catch or do everyday activities around the house or at work.*

The Rhythm you establish is your sport or activity is the Rhythm that will help you to decide. You should also try making decisions when you are not at your Still Point, and feel the difference between being decisive and indecisive.

Letting Go

THE FINAL STAGE of decision-making involves letting go. The experience you feel as you begin to act has at its core a sense of letting go, of letting things happen by getting out of your own way. You make no attempt at external control here, and have no concern whatsoever about results. The process takes care of everything. To get an idea of what this feeling is like for you, try the following exercise.

EXERCISE 4:2 *Prepare for a throw or shot that causes you considerable difficulty. Close your eyes. Feel your heart rate decrease. Your breathing should be calm and quiet. Wait for the change from this moment of stillness to when your heart rate and breathing are about to rise. Just at the moment you sense this change, bring back your club, racquet, or hand. Keep your eyes closed. Step away if you don't experience this feeling. Repeat the procedures again until you feel these changes. In this way, you will learn just how prepared you are to act. For the best results, try this exercise where you actually play, but it can be done at home or on the practice range as well. It is an exercise in* *"being involved," in creating your moment, your ritual. The key consists in keeping your eyes closed. By doing so, you focus not on results, but on yourself. You can use this exercise with other activities.*

Actions that flow with the graceful cycles of your Rhythm are, by their very nature, complete. You are left with the feeling that you have done your very best, and with the freedom to start a new challenge because the old one is in the past. Your actions were focused and didn't lose any power trying to get around walls of doubt, manipulation, or defending what you did. By letting yourself act, you took down the walls. With nothing to block them, your actions joined the wave to reach your goal, naturally and successfully. This is an experience I think we could and should get used to.

Release

W HEN YOU LET go, your actions were released to their fullest. Nothing was left behind. There is no way you can do things half-way by the time you are on the crest of the second wave. Common sense suggests that you would be exhausted if you gave your all! Here is another of those fascinating paradoxes of the Rhythm: instead of feeling fatigue, you are exhilarated, elated, delighted. Exhaustion comes only when you're gone half-way or less. Tiredness comes from fighting against yourself. It can also produce a profound lethargy that prevents you from trying again. You may recover from doing things this way, but it will be too late. None of this will happen if you follow your Rhythm because you can't get in your own way and won't spend energy fighting yourself.

You gain control of your mind by letting go and trusting. When you are able to do this, you become centered; your valuable time expands; and you create a movement of right consciousness and right action.

Once you have been in the trough and out again, you

have a responsibility to return. Each time you enter and
leave to go back into the world, you carry with you what
was learned at the Still Point. With this knowledge, you
can make the world a better place. Each rhythmic cycle
begins with excited preparation and ends with directed action. Throughout each cycle you will learn to trust yourself
more and more — and, at the same time, learn to let yourself go to be guided into action. At the action end of the
cycle, you will experience the release and focusing of
physical, emotional, and spiritual energies. Your actions
will seem to flow through you and out into the world:
guided, not forced. These are actions that you can trust and
need not fear defending.

5 The Excitement and the Discipline: Being Able to Concentrate

And I have felt
A presence that disturbs me with the joy
Of elevated thoughts; a sense sublime
Of something far more deeply interfused,
Whose dwelling is the light of setting suns,
And the round ocean and the living air,
And the blue sky, and in the mind of man:
A motion and a spirit, that impels
All thinking things, all objects of all thought,
And rolls through all things.

[William Wordsworth, quoted in Juan Mascaró, Lamps of Fire, 1972, p. 60]

Here we have a game that requires more calmness, judge-
ment, stolidity, and control than any other game ever
known — for the player here is at all times playing against
himself — his own weakness. And yet we have thousands
of players trying to learn it with frazzled nerves, with their
tempers unleashed, with their judgement wrecked, simply
because they haven't been able to control themselves, and
all the while they are wondering why it is they can't pos-
sibly "get back on their game."

[Jerome Travers, The Winning Shot, 1915, p. 52]

The ideal attitude is "controlled elan."

[Horace Hutchinson, Golf, 1890, p. 239]

THE PRESENCE that Wordsworth describes, the lack of it that Travers sees in so many people who try to play golf, and the wonderfully concise description given by Hutchinson have one thing in common: they all refer to a part of the Rhythm in each of us, the part concerned with concentration and inspiration. This part of the Rhythm prepares a relief pitcher to come out from the relative obscurity of the bullpen into the glare and pressures of the mound. It readies place-kickers and punters for that one moment when the game hangs in the balance. It enables figure skaters to be at their peak for their brief performance of 3 or 4 minutes. It guides you through those special moments of your life.

> *"It's tough sitting around all day waiting to do a small part," he said. "I deal with it all the time. You tend to lose your energy as the day wears on, and then when they finally call you for your scene, you already feel wiped out. The thing to remember is that the only moments that count are the moments when you're on camera. They're only a few moments out of the day, but they're the moments you're here for. So when the time comes, get your energy up and then just be yourself."*
>
> [John Diehl, who played Zito on "Miami Vice," in interview with Bob
> Greene, Esquire, July 1986, p. 76]

To many of us, concentration carries with it a number of negative misconceptions: (1) it is a fixed and rigid state; (2) it takes years of self-discipline to achieve it; (3) it comes and goes, and is beyond our control; (4) even if we can do it, we aren't sure what we can do with it; and (5) it is certainly not a pleasurable condition. Perhaps the singular belief about concentration that has hindered its attainment more than any other is that it takes a very long time to achieve this mental and physical state. The belief is also incorrect! To be able to concentrate, particularly under pressure, is to bring together two mental states that most of us believe are mutually exclusive — excitement and discipline. Yet definitions of concentration often include the words focus, rivet, unify, integrate, converge, undistracted, unswerving, complete, enthrallment, and raptness. When you are concentrating, you are learning how your emotions can be channelled to work for you by being disciplined enough to let your Rhythm guide you. At the same time, you are reinforcing your trust in yourself to make that leap into action without falling or losing your foothold. I will show you that concentrating takes far less time than you have believed, and that you do not have to do it for very long to produce the results you want.

For example, in a typical round of golf (if there is such a thing), which can take anywhere from 4½ to 6 hours to play, you actually have to concentrate for only 6 to 10 minutes spaced over the whole round. A baseball pitcher who throws an average of 120 to 130 pitches per game must concentrate for only 10 to 12 minutes. During a business day or a day at home, if you can concentrate for about 10 minutes, your day will be a success. The key is knowing when and how. And your Rhythm gives you that key. Stay in your Rhythm and you will know, at all levels, when and where and how!

Being Centered

T HE ACT OF concentrating can be accurately described as a state of awareness in which the following things converge.

1. You bring toward a common center an idea, an image, a decision.

EXERCISE 5:1 *Focus your breathing using one of the breathing exercises given earlier, gradually shift your attention to the center of your forehead.*

---

2. Your mental powers increase in strength as you focus more
and more on the center.

EXERCISE 5:2 *Continue with Exercise 5:1 but try to remain centered. Do not try to divert your thoughts or body, just try to focus on the center of your forehead.*

---

3. You will feel and see the various pieces of your thoughts,
ideas, images, and decisions coming closer and closer
together.

EXERCISE 5:3 *Continue with Exercises 5:1 and 5:2, trying to hold your focus for longer periods. (Do not do this exercise for more than 5 to 10 minutes at a time.)*

---

4. You will feel that all of what you have been focusing on
condense to one idea, image or decision.

EXERCISE 5:4 *After doing the above exercises, return to the following breathing exercise.*
  With your mouth slightly open, listen to the sound "HH" as you breath in. When you can hear this sound, focus your thoughts as you breathe in. As you practice, your thoughts will become absolutely clear.

---

5. You are still!

Concentration achieves two interdependent goals that are
essential in any life situation:

1. It removes the less valuable elements of the situation
and discards them; and

2. It reduces all the valuable parts to one understandable
and practical outcome.

Concentration makes certain demands of the ear, eye, memory, and imagination. It requires a person to adapt to a situation, or to a condition. These demands are made so that the strings of ideas and actions can be wound into one central string.

The Right Frame of Mind

I T WON'T DO you very much good if you are able to concentrate, but it happens to be on the wrong thing. The difference between a good and a great quarterback is the ability to pick up those cues from the opponent's defensive set that indicate what they are going to do next. A person who can do this quickly will be in a class by himself, as was Joe Namath of the Jets. In baseball recently, we've seen the re-emergence of "the hitter." Reasons advanced to explain this phenomenon ranged from a souped-up ball, to artificial turf, to shorter fences, and finally to less-capable pitchers. Hardly anyone dared to suggest that the hitters were reading the pitchers better. This form of "reading" comes down to being able to see the ball — that is, seeing the seams turn over so you can tell what type of pitch is on the way — and anticipating what the pitcher will throw. Ball clubs now have computer printouts that detail past pitching performance and try to predict what a pitcher will throw to a particular batter in a given situation. But someone still has to hit the ball, and they can't hit it if they don't "see" it. Seeing a ball involves (1) anticipating what a pitcher will throw, and (2) concentrating not on the pitcher but on the ball.

In the wonderful logic of baseball, anticipation and concentration have now become, "you wait for your pitch and when you get it, you'd better hit it." The best "waiters" are the best hitters because they anticipate when their pitch is coming and concentrate on the ball. They concentrate so well that they see the ball for a longer time before they hit it than players with poorer batting averages.

The person who performs well in goal or on the mound, at the office or at home, must be able to anticipate events, and concentrate at the proper time. Each of us, in one way or another, has learned that we can anticipate and concentrate, but there is a good deal of room for improvement.

Scientific studies have found that individuals have characteristic ways of looking at objects and events that are familiar to them. Our eyes follow a preferred path when we inspect or recognize a familiar object. Recognizing an object when it is encountered again involves matching past sensory impressions to the present one. The process takes time — often too much time to act appropriately. You could not wait for your pitch, match it with past pitches, and still have time to hit the ball. In the same way, if you took all the time necessary to match all your impressions each time you encountered a new situation, by the time you got around to doing anything, it would be too late. (Readings from Scientific American, *Mind and Behavior*, 1980; *Perception Mechanisms & Models*, 1972.)

Each of us takes longer to recognize complex objects or events than simpler ones; and, on average, it takes longer to recognize familiar objects than to reject non-familiar ones. For this reason, even if you "wait for your pitch," you may take longer than you thought to see it. Of course, this will not happen if you are also concentrating on the cues that distinguish that pitch from others.

Anticipation and Concentration: Keeping Your Eye on the Ball

YOU HAVE SOME personal behavioral habit or ritual that you have developed to initiate and maintain your concentration. These habits focus your attention in a special way so that you become aware of the range of implications and possible developments of your ideas. Feelings of anticipation pave the way for this new balance. Anticipating that something is going to happen enables you to focus and concentrate.

When you can see the slow dance of your golf ball, once it leaves the face of your putter and moves unerringly toward the hole as if it were being pulled by an invisible string — you can say you kept your eye on the ball.

When you can see your opponent's serve from the time it leaves the racquet, arching slowly over the net, until it leaves the strings of your racquet and speeds away — you have kept your eye on the ball.

When you have anticipated each move by the other party, had your counter-actions and straw men ready and waiting, and concluded the negotiations so that all parties gained — then you can say you kept your eye on the ball.

Countless experiences that happen every day give you the opportunity to bring together your abilities to concentrate and anticipate to the point that there is a maximum overlap between them.

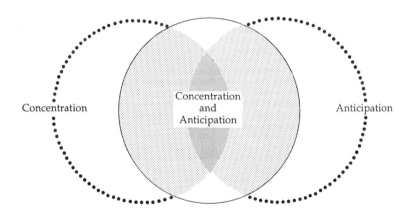

An unexpected, and definitely overlooked, benefit of concentration is that instead of seeing where things are and where they have been (which is considered to be an ordinary way of looking at the world), you begin to see the direction things are taking. This awareness builds slowly and steadily from being able to anticipate, to being able to anticipate and act, to understanding the probable pattern of events in the future. The more you practice getting yourself to your S.P. and beyond, the less anxious you become about what is going to happen because you can shape these things. You shape events because you can completely trust your own perceptions, inspirations, and instincts. As you gain more and more confidence, you move farther along the spokes of a great moving wheel toward its hub. Once you get there, you can see the whole cycle of change and can make the necessary adjustments as one series of events is replaced by another.

My inner feeling kept saying, "Let's do it a little bit better." Because there are really no limits. That's why I was so successful at swinging the bat. The discipline gave me a special kind of focus: I have been able to adjust my swing from one pitch to another, and even during the windup. God gave me the talent, and I had the desire and discipline to make the most of it.

[Rod Carew (one of only 16 major-league players in the history of the game to get 3,000 hits), quoted in Joe Flower, "Secrets of the Masters," 1987, p. 129]

"Keeping your eye on the ball" really means concentrating on the right cues while discarding the others, and anticipating what is going to happen. It means staying centered on what is important.

EXERCISE 5:5 *Stand over your golf ball; take your time to prepare to serve or make a throw; give yourself a time of quiet before starting on a project. Wait as long as you can with your eyes closed without being distracted. Keep practicing. Learn what your limits are and reduce them. Then, try the same thing with your eyes open; and with your eyes half open. These are exercises in staying balanced and centered.*

THE FUSION OF CONCENTRATION AND ANTICIPATION AT THE
STILL POINT

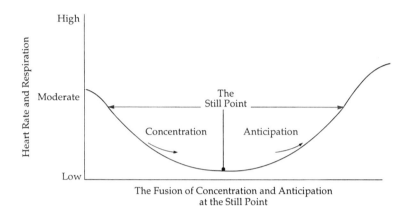

The Fusion of Concentration and Anticipation
at the Still Point

Concentration and anticipation are a natural part of the
cycle of your Rhythm. Both are achieved as you experience
and recognize the signposts of your S.P.

Learn to keep your eye on the ball using the sport or activity you enjoy or want to take up. Then you can learn to
keep an eye on another "ball," whether it be a personal
goal, a decision you have to make, or a solution to a
problem. By staying in Rhythm in sports, in business, or in
your home and social life, you can be assured that your
concentration and anticipation will be in synch with the
flow of the events around you.

Inspiration

WHEN YOU ARE concentrating, you can completely forget for a time that you have a body. Often the distractions that disrupt your concentration serve merely as
reminders that your body is still there.

I remember taking a series of exams for graduate school.

I was breezing through the afternoon tests (after completing three hours in the morning) until somehow the ticking of a clock penetrated my awareness. Before, there had been only the test and me; now there was this damned clock! Then I noticed a shapely leg, a growling in my stomach, the temperature of the room, and my concentration was lost.

Where there is a balance between mind and body, so that neither is forgotten, there is not need for disturbances, and you are free to concentrate. Initially, you may feel half-asleep and half-awake. In this twilight level between consciousness and the unconscious, streams of words and images seem to flow without regard to geography or common sense. But there is something to their pattern, something that is still hidden that attracts you. You can catch a glimpse of it here and there. You have a feeling that it *is* there. It continues to attract you. It seems to be taking you somewhere. Next, you may make a conscious effort to get a clear view of these movements, and to anticipate where they are heading next.

Then, after the wonder of discovery, you experience distractions, both inside and outside. You are dealing with the limitations you have lived with up to now. It's a necessary level to experience and go beyond. It's not only necessary; it's natural.

As you focus more and more, a familiar feeling of awareness comes over you. As a child you had the same feeling when you uncovered a great secret and decided to keep it to yourself for a little while. This is the moment of inspiration.

Your inspiration may begin in small waves of thoughts, ideas, and decisions. This is the music of your Rhythm: the music that gives life to your visions and fills you with the delight of knowing that what you are doing is right. Inspiration can also come over you in one powerful, flowing wave that, far from frightening you, takes you along with it on a dazzling ride. You may ride into the deepest reaches of your thoughts, then emerge again prepared to act.

Inspiration represents the beginning and end of a cycle of concentration. It is there at the first idea, and again at the outcome. In between, it becomes part of your Rhythm and can seem like a flash of sudden insight, unexplained by simple logic. Inspiration, then, is knowing you have uncovered a secret that makes things seem simple and complete where before they were confused and fragmented.

From the feeling of knowing a secret comes feelings of delight, because now you have the energy and trust to act on your new knowledge. Your emotions and intellect are working together to achieve what you know is right:

1. There is *integrity in your purpose*. You are committed to what you are doing, and you feel this is the best course;

2. You *don't get lost* and are able to stay on track in spite of the roadblocks, whether they stay in place or move around. You manage to get around them and get back to the path you choose;

3. You know very well *what has to be said and done and what doesn't*. You know what to disregard and what to pay attention to, and why.

EXERCISE 5:6 *This is a very straightforward exercise in what might be called applied inspiration, or not overlooking what you might ordinarily.*

Write your ideas down, no matter how practical or impractical they seem at first. Come back to them later and see how they have changed. I tell my students to write down all the ideas they have in class. You would be surprised how often these ideas have proven to be workable and profitable, personally and financially.

These three elements form the tone of your concentration, giving it a personal rhythm that produces inspiration.

The more you are able to master the particular discipline of concentration, the more inspired you can become. This is a discipline that is dynamic, fresh, and inventive. As you watch and absorb your own inner moves, you will know that you can do it again and again; and the realization that you can act on your feelings of inspiration encourages faith and confidence.

Anticipation, concentration, and inspiration constitute a heightened state of perception. In this state, we actually observe in advance and are able, as a consequence, to preclude actions that could be disruptive and prevent ourselves from being distracted. We are also able to take precautionary actions because we can see ahead. How often have you slowed down on a highway or changed lanes because you "felt something was going to happen"? Could you be a good chess player without anticipation and inspiration as companions? Most calls by sports officials — especially in sports such as ice hockey, basketball, and football — are actions based on anticipated happenings. Do you act on such feelings? Or do you disregard them?

The following exercise illustrates the essential differences between concentration and compulsion (we are capable of both, and are also influenced by how problems are presented to us).

EXERCISE 5:7   *Your task is to place a dot with a pencil in the centre of each circle on the next page. This exercise is highly related to your ability to take tests successfully.*

Complete as many circles as you can. When you stop, record the time you took doing the exercise and the number of clean hits.

Concentration Training: An Example

C AN YOU imagine yourself in goal with pucks coming at you at 100 mph or more, with everyone watching you? Can you picture yourself in one of the most challenging and pressure-filled positions in sports?

Could you imagine yourself doing this if you were blindfolded?

○ ○ ○ ○ ○ ○ ○ ○

○ ○ ○ ○ ○ ○ ○ ○

○ ○ ○ ○ ○ ○ ○ ○

○ ○ ○ ○ ○ ○ ○ ○

○ ○ ○ ○ ○ ○ ○ ○

○ ○ ○ ○ ○ ○ ○ ○

○ ○ ○ ○ ○ ○ ○ ○

○ ○ ○ ○ ○ ○ ○ ○

○ ○ ○ ○ ○ ○ ○ ○

○ ○ ○ ○ ○ ○ ○ ○

○ ○ ○ ○ ○ ○ ○ ○

What if the instructions for the exercise had read, "This is an exercise in how compulsive you are"? How many circles would you have attempted? How much time would you have taken? Try this on your friends and colleagues with different instructions and you will see the differences.

You can also try a variant of this exercise. In this case, your task is to draw a line between each of the printed lines on the next page, without touching them. Again, as in the circle exercise, record the time and the number of clean lines.

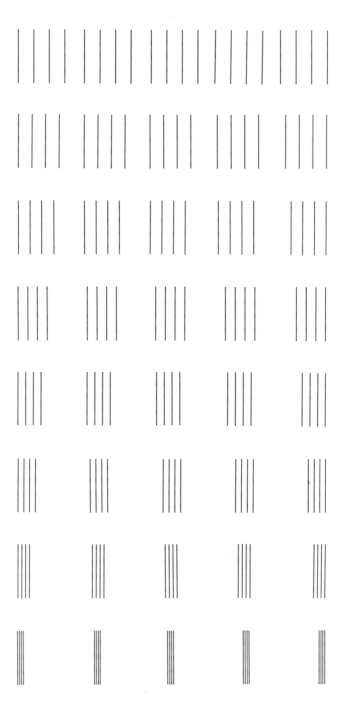

Bernie Parent claims that goalies must be at least a bit crazy. Would you answer the advertisement below if it appeared in the newspaper?

HELP WANTED
POSITION AVAILABLE

A small, dynamic organization requires the services of an individual to protect a 24-square-foot area with a netted backing from being penetrated by a black cylindrical object 7.62 cm (in diameter) x 2.54 cm (in height), weighing 156-170 grams. This object can approach the area from a variety of angles and distances at speeds of 100 mph or more. The working environment demands the presence of members of a competitive organization, and a number of officials and witnesses. The individual hired for this job will be helped by two to four others with varying levels of skill and enthusiasm. Must be willing to handle pressure and accept failure for the whole organization. Must also be able to function at a consistently high level of performance under conditions of restricted mobility. Equipment (i.e., uniforms, pads, gloves, sticks, masks, etc.) will be provided, as well as a generous hospitalization plan. Salary and other benefits are negotiable, depending upon experience. Send resumé in confidence to Box 247, care of this paper.

Let's assume that we do hire some promising rookies. Can we give them some training in concentration in a controlled situation before we put them into a game?

Sport psychologists, physiologists, coaches, and even players have agreed that you cannot train to improve concentration. This stance usually boils down to "either you have it or you don't, and the only ones who have it have been 'in the pressure cooker many times'." I guess I was just too dense to believe such compelling arguments. After a year and a half of trying, I convinced some goaltenders to try a challenge I had devised. Up to the time that we carried out our training, research had shown that experienced goaltenders could stop, on average, nine shots out of ten fired by a player at the blue line, even when the puck was travelling at over 90 mph. Yet these same goaltenders were only able to stop two out of ten pucks propelled by a puck-shooting machine, also positioned at the blue line at a mere 50 mph.

This research suggested to me that prior to shooting a puck, a player provides cues for the goaltender. By concentrating on these cues, goalies can "anticipate the shot," or look into the future, and be in a position to stop the puck or deflect it away from the net area. Even though the information precedes the actual shot by only a fraction of a second, the fact that such information is available seems to make a significant difference in performance.

The next step was to test the hypothesis that effective performance is strongly related to a goaltender's ability to concentrate on whatever cues are available, either internal or external, in various game situations, and then act on this information. This ability to concentrate would be hidden from others, but would show up in a knack of anticipating where the shot will come from.

To give goalies an idea of how well or poorly they could concentrate, I set up the following situation. A goalie would be put in net, with full equipment, while being monitored for heart rate and respiration. The best shooters on the team would take 40 shots among them. They would select the shots and the order. They would skate in from center ice, and could glide in or skate in hard. They could do just about anything they wanted to except take a slap shot.

For the first sequence of 40 shots, the goaltender would be blindfolded. The shooters would call out "blue line" when they reached it, and give no other clues to the goalie. After a 10-minute break, a second sequence of 40 shots would begin; this time the goalie would be fully sighted.

Now, put yourself in this situation. The best shooters on your team are going to be taking shots on net, and you cannot see where they are. The only clue you will hear is "blue line." What is your heart rate now? As you try to listen to find out where your team-mate is on the ice, is your heart rate going up or down? The player is ready to shoot; what is your heart rate?

Heart-rate measurements taken over five-second intervals — at the time the shooter was at center ice, passing the blue line, and releasing the puck, and during the time in which the goaltender was preparing for the next shot — were compared for blindfolded and sighted conditions, and by shot type (for instance, lateral right, lateral left, deke right, deke left). The results of the study can be summarized as follows:

1. Heart rates taken under non-visual (blindfolded) conditions were roughly 8% to 15% lower than rates taken under sighted conditions. These heart-rate differences provide clear evidence for the greater concentration achieved by goaltenders under non-visual conditions. Heart rates and respiration slow down when you are concentrating and rise when you are anxious.

2. Heart rates were associated with the type of shot taken. Higher rates were found to be related to those shots that goaltenders reported, prior to the testing, that they had difficulty in handling. We learn to experience anxiety with specific situational cues. But we can unlearn it as well. Those shots reported to be relatively easy to defend against were associated with lowered rates. Under the non-visual condition heart rates were also found to be consistently higher for the more difficult shot types; even though the goalie could not "see" the shots taken in the ordinary way, he was anticipating it — and he was more often right than wrong.

3. Heart rates during the recovery period (that is, the period in which the goaltender was preparing for the next shot) were not significantly different from those rates taken at the time the preceding shot was taken. Changes were on the order of 1 to 3%. Such a finding suggest that goaltenders may not really achieve physiological recovery. Increased heart rates were noted

especially after a difficult shot had been taken. Non-visual mean heart rates during recovery remained consistently lower than sighted rates (127.25 beats per minute versus 138.78 beats). This result, if it holds up over the long run, may serve to indicate that goaltenders under non-visual conditions can "recover" more efficiently than under sighted conditions.

4. The pattern of goalie heart-rate changes as the shooter progressed from center ice, to the crossing of the blue line, to the taking of a shot was most interesting and intriguing, since it argued against common sense.

   (a) Under sighted conditions, mean heart rates increased from center ice (130.14 beats per minute), to the blue line (132.01 beats per minute), to the taking of a shot (137.9 beats per minute).

   (b) Under non-visual conditions, heart rates from center ice (117.59 beats per minute), to the blue line (118.21 beats per minute), to the taking of a shot (111.28 beats per minute) were considerably lower. This heart-rate change reflects a pattern of remaining still and centered.

After five weeks of training, sighted goaltenders' heart rates were lowered by 7%. After three weeks of this type of training, goaltenders, on average, allowed 3.5 shots of the first 34 taken, and 6.0 shots per 40 shots taken in a 1-on-0 situation. When playing actual games, their goals-against average dropped about 17%.

No one really expected a blindfolded goalie to stop a puck, but it did happen. For those of you who remain skeptical, I have put on videotape some of these training sessions, and you may write to me if you would like to see it for yourself. What we did expect was that after each blindfolded session, the goalies' "other senses" would be heightened, along with their ability to concentrate and anticipate in pressure situations (for instance, a good deal of traffic around the net). Their performance improved quickly and they were able to maintain the gains. They described the experience of being blindfolded and then being able to see as follows:

When I couldn't see I tried to listen to the sound of the shots, but they glided in sometimes. The players hit the ice with their sticks, which threw me off. I really don't know how it actually happened but I stopped trying to listen. I don't know how to describe it but it was as if a hand was pushing me out of the net toward the shooter. I just went with the feeling. Somehow I just knew it was right. I'll tell you, 10 minutes of this is like playing two periods. When the blindfold came off, everything was clear. I could see where the shot was going to come from. I felt like I was hardly moving. I was just going with my feelings. It was as if I wrote the play down and the guys were doing it.

[a compilation of comments by goalies]

EXERCISE 5:8   *Read this sentence out loud:*

A DIAMOND IN THE THE ROUGH HIDES ITS TRUE WORTH.

Now read it again. Did you do it correctly? Did you see the second "the"?

Being Creative

Before the battle at Wimbleton was 30 minutes old, Becker had hit one shot off his knees and another flat on his stomach after belly-flopping while lunging. In a magnificent effort, he managed to stab a backhand that cleared the net.

*Early in the second set, in a stunning improvisation, . . .
rather than chipping a weak backhand, Becker spon-
taneously changed hands, using his left hand to flick a
forehand cross-court. Becker later said that "using my left
hand was the only chance I had to make that shot. I
thought, let's try and it went in. It just came over me at
that moment to play it left!"*

[McCabe, Nora, June 24. 1987. Becker, Lendl handy victors.

Globe and Mail, *Toronto, p. D2.]*

*Since one of [intrapreneurs'] most basic tools is daydream-
ing, their natural inclination in any spare moment is to
play over a new business opportunity in their mind's eye,
considering the many different ways to go forward and the
barriers they might encounter along each path. Because
they foresee barriers, intrapreneurs can plan ways around
them before being locked in a death struggle with an un-
workable situation.*

[Roy Rowan, The Intuitive Manager, *1986, p. 124]*

Creative problem-solving has two requirements:

1. Don't be attached to one idea or one way;

2. Don't imitate.

In some ways, we are creative in our approach to solving
problems, and in other ways, we seem to be stuck with
using methods that make us feel comfortable, but are not
very successful. Life means having to deal with problems
— different ones at different times and unfamiliar ones
every so often. Solutions that have worked for a loved one,
close friend, or colleague, sometimes don't work so well
for us. The physician, lawyer, or broker your friend swears
by may turn out to be clod. You can't stand the counsellor
who helped one of your colleagues. The consultant who
did such a good job for a similar company doesn't have a
handle on your firm's problems.

If your mind and body are experiencing turbulence,

you cannot be creative. All you can do is try to get through this rough period. Creativity comes when there is calmness; and when there is calmness, you can choose. A creative decision leaves nothing to do but act. There is an absolute bond here, and a correct one, between thoughts and actions. After you act, you can begin anew. This is what a creative decision leaves you with — a feeling of completeness and the opportunity to start on a new project.

To be creative is to be completely attentive and relaxed, tranquil and without fear. Through reaching your Still Point comes the realization that you know the right techniques and know yourself.

I am not trying to play down conscious thinking. Instead, I am trying to show you that you can base decision-making on different levels of awareness.

Being creative means being able to pass freely, in both directions, from a superficial level of understanding through deeper and deeper levels. There should be no roadblocks in the way of these exchanges. This doesn't mean you get bombarded by every stray image and idea, but only that you can draw from these levels when you need to. You can learn what each has to offer in a particular situation. Creativity never wastes any effort on trying to control results: it is totally oriented toward the process. When it is really working for you, when your so-called "creative juices" are "flowing," they are flowing to your Rhythm.

When you establish your Rhythm, mind and body become fully integrated and actions move in a natural sequence. Such integration produces a level of awareness that reveals the essence of problems rather than just confirming their presence. This integration can be achieved whether you are playing or working. Any activity in which you make decisions at your Still Point strengthens your mind and spirit.

Problem-Solving

EXERCISE 5:9 *In the 11 problems to follow, your task is to measure out the amount of milk asked for by each customer. You can use any or all of the empty containers (A, B, or C) given to you. You should take no longer than 2½ minutes for each problem. Solve the problems in order and write down your answer and how long it took you to solve each problem. Do not go any further until you have worked on the entire set of problems.*

| | Empty Containers (Capacity in Quarts) | | | Number of Quarts the |
Problem	A	B	C	Customer Needs
1	29	3		20
2	21	127	3	100
3	14	163	25	99
4	18	43	10	5
5	9	42	6	21
6	20	59	4	31
7	23	49	3	20
8	15	39	3	18
9	28	76	3	25
10	18	48	4	22
11	14	36	8	6

[from Abraham Luchins, "Mechanization in Problem Solving," Psychology Monograph, Vol 54, No. 6, 1942. In the Public Domain.]

The problems in Exercise 5:9 have been used for over 40 years to demonstrate how people can become so intrigued with *one* way of solving a problem they don't see any other, more economical ones.

Problem 1 can be solved by the formula "A - 3B." Fill Container A (29 quarts); then from it fill Container "B" (3 quarts) three times, leaving 20 quarts in Container A. Problems 2, 3, 4, 5, and 6 can be solved using the formula

"B - A - 2C." Here, you first fill Container B, then from its contents fill Container A once and Container C twice. Problems 7, 8, and 9 can be solved more directly and economically: "A - C," "A + C," and "A - C," respectively.

If you used the more direct solutions, then you have overcome the bias set up by the first series of problems. This is a bias many others have not been able to overcome. It means that your decision-making was efficient and correct; and that you can adjust to changing conditions.

If you continued to use the earlier solution ("B - A - 2C"), you solved problems 7 and 8, but it took longer than it should have. Problem 9, however, could not be solved using "B - A - 2C"; this certainly caused some trouble.

Solutions that have worked in the past may not work so well in the present. Beware of the repeated use of the same method to solve your problems. This can blind you to other ways. Don't let habit become master. Instead, master your habits.

A king had two sons, both of whom he loved dearly. He could not choose between the two as to which of them would succeed him. With the assistance of a court advisor (this was before the days of lawyers), he devised a test for the boys. The winner would be the next king.

Each son was to choose a horse and travel to a city a day's ride away. From there a very special race would take place: the son whose horse came through the gates of the castle last would be the next king. The young men were sent off.

Days went by, then weeks; no sign of either son. So the king sent his advisor to find them. He found them lounging around the city, uncertain of what to do. He whispered a message from the king to each of them. They ran to the horses and raced toward the castle.

What was the king's message to his sons?

ANSWER: Go fetch your brother's horse.

EXERCISE 5:10 *Decision-making is by no means a mystical experience. This exercise illustrates several key factors in learning how to use it.*

a. See details and their interrelationships vividly
   Could you construct the object shown in Figure 5-1?

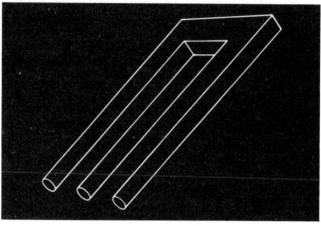

Figure 5-1
This is what is called an "irrational figure." It can only exist on paper and is not physically possible to construct.

[D. H. Schuster, 1964. "A new ambiguous figure: a three stick clevis."
                        American Journal of Psychology, 77, 673.]

b. Focus on what you need to.
   Now look at Figure 5-2. Which man is larger?
   Look at Figure 5-3. Which circle is larger?   Figure 5-2

The three men are the same size. They appear to increase in size because of their different locations within a system of converging lines.

[This figure is based upon the "Titchner circles," as appeared in W. Wendt, 1898, 'Die geometrisch optischen Täuschungen; Abhandl. math phys. der sachs ges. WISS., 24, 53-178.]

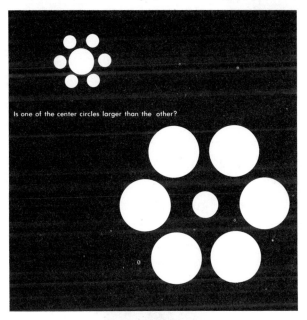

Is one of the center circles larger than the other?

Figure 5-3

They are exactly the same. They seem to be unequal because of the contrast in size of the circles surrounding them. This illusion shows you that if you pay attention to what is being asked, you will not be tricked. Try to focus on the two centre circles, blocking out the others. Also, try this illusion with a group.

[This illusion is based upon the work of W. Von Bezold, 1884. "Eine perpektivische Täuschung"; Poggend. Annlen, 23, 351-2; and W. Ittleson & F. Kilpatrick, 1952. "Experiment in perception," Scientific American, 185, 50-55.]

c. *See the* appearance of interrelationships *as if you are look-ing at a familiar situation or object for the first time.*

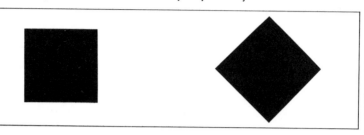

The square and the diamond are two familiar shapes. The two figures shown are identical. Yet, their appearance is different. We call one a square and the other a diamond.

Figure 5-4

d. *Have* people and problems revealed to you in an intui-tive way *that you know is correct.*

Who do you see in Figure 5-5?

Figure 5-5

Did you see the young or old woman first?

Did your perception change as you looked at the picture? Your feelings?

YOUNG GIRL-OLD WOMAN was brought to the attention of psychologists by Edwin G. Boring in 1930. Created by cartoonist W. E. Hill, it was originally published in Puck *in 1915 as "My Wife and My Mother-in-law." The young woman's chin is the old woman's nose.*

[*Boring, E. 1930. "A New Ambiguous Figure."* American Journal of
Psychology, 42, 444.]

I have used illusions to show you how you make decisions and how you can be tricked. Some illusions work because, like good magicians, they deflect your attention from the essential details. Parts become wholes, and wholes become parts; and parts can turn out to be the opposite of what they started out to be. Other illusions work because you spend too much time looking at them. Illusions are one of the oldest and most interesting ways of learning how to see and decide.

In all decision-making, center on the question, remain still, and you will see clearly. If not, you open yourself up to being tricked. Even without having an illusion in front of you, you may find yourself misguided.

EXERCISE 5:11 *a. Pay attention to your feelings, to how your body is reacting. Do not focus on the outcome.*
Focus on the pause between in-breath and out-breath. At this instant, your feelings are separated from outcome, and outcome from feelings. At this instant, you can focus on either one or both and make a decision.

b. Let your attention move about, consolidate, and move on again.
Look at some object. Slowly withdraw your sight from it; now withdraw your thoughts from it. Now focus on your problem, and decide.

c. Move beyond what has been called logic.
Take a deep breath. Before you exhale, one thought will come forward and strengthen as you exhale. Center your attention between your eyebrows. Then let your mind wander. When one thought becomes clear again, you will know it is right.

d. Make being calm a familiar experience for you. You will sense and know the correct time to act. This is not a sixth sense, but an element of the process of natural, rhythmic decision-making.

6 The Management of Time: Real Magic

No two days are ever exactly alike: some are foggy, rainy, some dry or windy; and this endless variety greatly enhances the beauty of the universe. And even so precisely is it with man, who, as the ancient writers have said, is a miniature of the world, for he is never long in any one condition, and his life on earth flows by like the mighty waters, heaving and tossing with an endless variety of motion; one while raising him on high with hope, another plunging him low in fear; now turning him to the right with rejoicing, then driving him to the left with sorrows; and no single day, no, not even one hour, is entirely the same as any other of his life.

[St. Francois de Sales I, quoted in Juan Mascaró,
Lamps of Fire, 1972, pp240-241]

The Illusion of Time Management

YOUR RHYTHM and how you relate to time are interdependent. Changes in one bring about changes in the other. As you slow down, so does the flow of time. As you speed up and become anxious and tense, the flow of time seems to compress, so that you feel there is less of it left to you to use. Time is not something to be managed like your budget, family vacations, and business meetings. Time is one of the fundamental mysteries of our lives, and has been a source of fascination and frustration throughout recorded history. Attempting to manage such a powerful, pervasive, and fluid force is like trying to navigate a small canoe successfully across the Atlantic at the height of a major storm.

The idea of time management wrongly assumes that time is "out there somewhere," beyond each of us and that, by putting it into little boxes, in expensive memo books, we can capture it. However, I hope to show in this chapter that there is no *one* time; rather, there are time zones, both geographic and personal. The illusion of time management is that by utilizing a series of techniques you can become a good manager. This is simply not true. Only by understanding and managing yourself can you learn how to use time and make it your ally.

Time and your metabolism enjoy an intricate and intimate bond. Once you understand your relationship to time, almost any sensible technique can be applied. By understanding the simple processes first, you will come to know all the processes. No special drug or so-called expert can give you the knowledge of time; you must learn how to acquire this knowledge yourself.

Early Time

As YOUNG CHILDREN, we have little or no adult-like awareness of time as measured by electronic or mechanical devices. Time blends into the endless magic of childhood, measured only by play, hunger, sleep, and dreams. Time is incredibly elastic, fluid, and expansive, and we experience its movements in a direct, personal way.

In the middle years of childhood (from age 6 through age 8) parents and school combine resources to teach us about clock time. Suddenly, days shorten, nights lengthen, feelings of being hungry fall out of synch with mealtimes, and our parents' age becomes a source of anxiety. We no longer hold the secret of time; it is held by those little machines hanging on walls and placed on our wrists.

Punishments and rewards appear for being late or on time. Our first wristwatch signals the end of childhood: we have now replaced our personal internal time with this contraption. From that day on, our relationship to time is altered. That day also marks the death of our illusion that time is not inside this gadget (no matter how expensive or sophisticated it might be). The exercises in the section "Playing with Times," later in this chapter, may help you to remember that time resides within us, and that we still have the ability to flex and bend it to our rhythms. All that is needed is a little practice. In Appendix C, you will find a brief history of our relationship to time, and how we have tried to capture it.

Clock Time

ANYTHING THAT moves, flows, consumes or can be consumed has been used as a measure of time. Movement and change became the fundamental bases for all our measures of time. The sundial represented a clear attempt to break down the day into regular units. The shadow of the sun became an early and universal measurement guide. (Sundial time also provided the Romans with the world's first time-and-motion study: it was believed that a soldier could march 20 miles in 5 summer hours.) Unfortunately, sundial time is difficult to compare in different seasons as the number of sunlight hours changes—and of course, it proves useless at night. So the next logical step—other than using the moon, which also alters in appearance—was to use something that moved independently of daytime hours. Water clocks became fashionable. Roman courts used them to ensure that lawyers would have equal time. Unfortunately the holes through which water escaped suffered some erosion, so jewels were placed around their edges, rendering them status symbols: apparently the jewelled water clock was the forerunner of today's Rolex.

Movement clocks used the motion of sand from one place to another to measure time. But their owners were forced to get up during the night to turn the hourglass over. The burning rate of aromatic candles or incense provided an aesthetic version of time measurement.

Our need to measure time during the dark hours and to divide it into smaller, more equal and accurate portions ultimately led to the mechanization of clocks. In the fourteenth century, the early forms of mechanical clocks appeared: they sounded the passage of time with chiming bells, rather than showing it by movements on a dial. Weight-driven mechanisms that struck a bell after a designated interval were eventually replaced by the rhythmic tick-tock of uniformity, and still later by the humming of electronic gadgetry.

Mechanization divided time into separate movements that no longer flowed, and extended the day into the night. Nature had been harnessed and standardized, but who won? Instead of being the victors, we seem to have become the victims of our historical desire to control and contain time. Instead of becoming independent of this measured time, we have adjusted our lives to it.

The clock is a "Western" phenomenon. Some have called it the "mother of all machines." Clocks caused the word "punctuality" to appear in our language in the eighteenth century, and by the nineteen century, time was no longer a solely public event to be heard only in town squares: it was now private as well. People could carry time on their wrists or in their pockets. Time now had the power to cause anxiety. To find out how much time anxiety is affecting *you* right now, take a few minutes to complete the Time Anxiety Scale in Appendix A.

What Is Anxiety about Time?

A colleague of mine was making a telephone call and the operator had put him on hold; he turned to me with a kind of mournful expression on his face and said, "Do you know what I'm feeling right now?" And because of the intensity of his feeling, I did. He was feeling that a few precious moments of his life were going by while he was holding onto this telephone; this black inanimate object was now the source of his anxiety about the irretrievability of time, his understanding that with each passing moment there would be one less.

Anxiety about time contains four major aspects:

1. An intellectual and emotional reaction to the belief that time is independent of your existence;

2. A concern about physical changes due to the passage of time;

3. A concern over how the flow of time changes—the faster it flows, the greater the concern; and

4. A concern about what the future will bring.

In our society, probably no better illustration of the experience of time anxiety exists than the "mid-life crisis." The mid-life period carries with it an awareness of aging, of changing roles: children are growing up, parents are growing older. We sense the approaching or imminent death of our parents and know that soon we will be taking their place. Mid-life is also a kind of second adolescence where conceptions of personal mortality change. Statistics show increased use of drugs, a resurgence of the need to succeed, and bouts of depression. This stage can also represent a healthy preparation for the transition to the period of old age. It has been suggested by many researchers that the mid-life crisis begins in one's late twenties, peaks in the thirties, and extends through the forties. Inadequate handling of the problems that arise in mid-life can precipitate accidents, traumatic neurosis, physical illness, drug addiction, alcoholism, mild or severe depression, and suicide. (R.N. Butler and M.I. Lewis, *Aging and Mental Health*, 1977). The traditional techniques for coping with the problems of mid-life are denial and projection. Denial involves avoidance of the problems in their entirety; projection on the other hand implies that the problems are not ours but are confined to those around us. Implicit in the mid-life crisis is a shift in time-order perspective. A particularly conspicuous feature of middle age entails restructuring our outlook in terms of *time left to live*, rather than *time since birth*. Not only do we reverse the direction we face, but we develop an awareness that the time left to us is finite.

Another characteristic of this mid-life period is the emergence of a "now-or-never" attitude. For the middle-aged person, wishes that were set aside for such considerations as family, reputation, or career must now either be given up or grasped quickly. Choices may lead to satisfaction or they can be disastrous, but the feeling of "urgency" remains constant.

It's like I betrayed that part of me. It's been waiting so long that it has to have a chance now or else it will be too late.
[the comments of a 45-year-old physician who wanted to give up his practice to become an anthropologist]

Mid-life dilemmas do not always lead to stagnation. They can lead to a realistic life review, for this is a period in which people can ask themselves what their lives have come to and what they are going to do in the time remaining. Although the central task of mid-life can be painful, avoiding it can be worse. Those people who age most successfully in this stage, with little psychological discomfort and with no loss of effectiveness, seem to be those who calmly invert their previous values, now putting the use of their "heads" above the use of their "hands," both as a standard for self-evaluation and as a chief resource for solving life's problems. Essentially mid-life seems to mean that we are no longer in a position to squander our resources; as a result, time takes on a strange new dimension—the time behind us expands out and away from us, while the time in front compresses. Robert Kastenbaum has called this phenomenon "the foreshortened life perspective" and has noted that it is also characteristic of the elderly. (*Geriatrics*, 1969, pp. 126—133)

Many of us suffer in our middle years from an inability to make any sense of our lives. Although mid-life presents an ideal time for review, many of us avoid the confrontation by devoting our attention to bodily functions and health worries. Perhaps we convince ourselves that if only this or that physical symptom were eliminated, we would be as youthful as ever. We may struggle with the mid-life crisis in part because of the "conspiracy of silence" surrounding the phenomenon itself. Little attention has been given to it, especially when so many experience it as a normal and significant part of life. Even publications such as Gail Sheehy's *Passages* have tended to pay much more attention to the stages and phases of development than to the unique and personal decisions made during mid-life. Reviewing your life signifies maturity and health; so if we can't review our lives in mid-course, how are we to do so in our later years?

The mid-life dilemma for most people consists in the inability to understand the direction they're going in and the direction they've come from. Mid-life affects each of us in different ways, but commonly involves changes in our perceptions of time, of our ourselves, and of others. It is a mistake to believe that such changes only take place during the years from 40 to 55. The dilemmas, the shifts in perception can happen many times throughout our lifespan. We may see fit at this particular time in our development to focus in on those years. But these same problems can arise in our twenties or thirties, and may persist into our sixties, seventies and beyond. The dilemmas of the so-called mid-life period are the dilemmas of living.

EXERCISE 6:1 *Take out a piece of paper and draw a line or any other configuration to represent your life. On this line, mark off events that were of importance to you and your age at the time. Then go beyond your present age and project events to come. This exercise should be done more than once. It is a good exercise to come back to as you remember past events or project further events into the future.*

This is your resumé, not for any job, but for your life. This exercise will give you an idea of how time and events are interlinked as you grow and experience.

You might find that during your teen years there were a number of "first experiences": your first love, cigarette, job, car. As you grew older, fewer first-time experiences appeared, as more socially defined events began to dominate—for example, setting career and educational goals, making plans for a family, beginning to set the groundwork for financial security. You may even come up against unexpected barriers as you try to fill in the events of your life: perhaps the years between 5 and 8 seem to be a blur; could your early twenties really have been completely consumed with friends and school or work? As you return to the Life Line again, you will remember more and rediscover those lost years. And what of the future? What do you see for yourself and your loved ones? The Life Line exercise is about the early, present, and future time of your life—how you have spent your time and how you think you will. It gives you the pattern of your life along a very personal time continuum.

Anxiety about time can also function in some rather mystifying and healing ways that very often defy common sense. For example, picture yourself falling from a great height. Your parachute has failed to open and so has your reserve chute. The earth comes up at you with ever-increasing size and ferocity. Or your rope has broken and you are falling from a magnificent cliff. The side of the mountain races past you as your fall accelerates. What is going through your mind?

Near-Death Experiences

BRUCE GREYSON and Ian Stevenson, (1980) collected 78 reports of such experiences from three sources: letters to a national magazine from respondents who had read an article on near-death experiences, responses to announcements of interest in studying such cases in professional newletters and magazines, and communications from people who knew of their long-standing interest in the nature of death experiences. For each of these cases a first-hand written report or tape-recorded account was collected, as was questionnaire and interview material. In addition, the researchers examined medical records that were relevant to each of the near-death experiences.

At the time of their experiences, 27% of those in the sample were 18 years and younger; 32% were between 18 and 35 years old; and 40% were 35 years or older. Of the subjects, 63% were women; 47% were married, 40% were single, 12% were separated, widowed, or divorced. In 80% of the cases, medical personnel were present during or immediately after the experience: 40% of the experiences were precipitated by physical illness; 37% by traumatic injury; 13% by surgical operation, 7% in childbirth; and 4% by the ingestion of drugs. In 47% of the reports, some type of drug or alcohol was taken on the day of the experience. A full 67% of the interviewees reported that their near-death experience lasted for more than an hour.

A near-death experience often involves an out-of-body episode. The feeling of viewing one's physical body from outside was reported in 75% of Greyson and Stevenson's cases—and for 96% of this group, the actual leaving of the body was reported to be instantaneous and rather easy. Out of the 78 people in this study, 50% reported some sense of unity with nature, 37% the sense of God within themselves; 43% had the apparent memory of a previous life; 29% sensed auras; and 24% stated that they had communication with the dead.

In 31% of the cases, the reports included the description of passing through a tunnel, and in 57% of the cases some sort of "point of no return" was reached—suggesting that these people somehow approached the boundary between life and death. For our purposes here, perhaps the most significant finding from studies of the near-death experience is *the displacement of time*, which was reported by 79% of these subjects. For example, 54% of the group reported that time seemed to pass more slowly than usual. This apparent slowing of time is also associated with the experience of unusual visual phenomena, such as lights and auras, which were reported by 48% of the subjects and seemed to occur predominantly during the evening. An awareness of the rapid passage of time constitutes a sizable component of anxiety about death, accounting for about 12% of such anxiety. However, those individuals who reported distortions in their sense of time did not report anxiety about their death, though 52% of the subjects in the Greyson and Stevenson study reported that they believed they were actually dying during their near-death experience. In other words, the sensation of the slowing of time seems to check one's anxiety about death. Another possible source of anxiety about death experience might be the idea of having our life flash before us, with every tiny detail, every personal event, projected on a panoramic screen. Greyson and Stevenson reported such "panoramic memory" among 27% of their subjects; in keeping with their sense of time displacement, such memories did not seem to occur in any given or logical sequence, but rather all at one, in a simultaneous display or review of their lives.

The near-death experience was reported to be a very positive emotional experience by 15% of those going through it. The experience was mildly positive for another 40%, while 45% felt it either to be neutral or mildly negative. None of the subjects in this particular study reported their near-death experience to be very negative. A positive emotional effect was found to be strongly related to the degree to which subjective time was distorted. Evidently, the more one's personal sense of time slows down, the more positive the near-death experience feels. For those who actually believed that they were going to die, the positive emotional repercussions were even greater.

Of course, we must be careful in generalizing the results of such studies, as this is a highly selective sample and certainly does not represent a cross-section of the North American population. But even in this small non-random study, we can see that a sense of the slowing down of personal time reduces anxiety during near-death experiences.

In most reports of such experiences, a positive rather than negative feeling tends to persist.

Slowing Time

THOUGHTS AND actions that are experienced as being slow contain no unnecessary parts, links, or points of tension. Such thoughts and actions cannot be easily undone because they are so simple, so complete. Mechanical, rational, and other forms of analysis are rendered unnecessary, for they only make things more artificial.

Natural power always appears slow to observers—fluid, and beautifully executed. Perception of the real strength of these movements is reduced because no disconnected parts or changes of tempo disrupt the flow. Observers don't see the wasted effort because there isn't any. The grace of these movements hides their true worth. It creates a wonderful illusion that protects the secrets behind their success: an illusion that power and effectiveness are not there, when in fact they are!

Complicated, disjointed, unnaturally hurried behavior always seems faster than it really is. Observers don't see the hidden, wasted effort; instead, they see speed, because each change of tempo produces an erroneous overall impression that useful energy is being created. In each movement, from one split-second to the next, there is an invisible loss of timing, of power. This is a fundamental part of the "paradox of power."

Power cannot exist if there is no unity, no rhythm between thought and action. Hurried connections between the two can only work if luck is on your side. When unnecessary speed takes over, even potential self-control becomes lost. Speed replaces successful strategies with frustrating and harmful ones. For example, too many people deal with job stress by working harder and faster. But this strategy only creates more stress leading to a cycle of working even harder, even faster—which ends in exhaustion or worse.

Batters in a hitting slump tend to swing harder, which

leads them farther from their natural rhythm. To get more distance on their drives, golfers swing faster and faster. Bowlers and pitchers throw harder and try to direct the ball. Whenever they speed up, athletes sacrifice accuracy, ruin their timing, or lose distance.

The essence of the paradox of power consists in this: being slow is more powerful than being fast. Fluid, slow, well-timed thoughts and actions are powerful, natural, and effortless. Paradoxically, power is not felt as being powerful, it is felt as being natural.

A sweeping, graceful motion imparts a maximum exchange of energy to the object or obstacle it sets out to move. Being in Rhythm ensures a maximum exchange. *Decisions made during the Still Point further guarantee maximum exchange from thoughts into actions.* The quietness and timeless intensity reached during the Still Point ensure correct action.

Use the "being slow" exercises that follow to familiarize yourself with the feeling of natural power.

EXERCISE 6:2 *The goal in these exercises is to be slow, while maintaining a balance between feelings and actions. You will see that by being slow, you actually gain power. Why? Because your natural Rhythm is being strengthened, as is your timing, and you get better.*

The exercises are designed to fit into four general categories: hitting, targeting, moving, and protecting. Select the one you are most interested in or comfortable with.

Hitting: *This category includes such sports as: tennis, squash, handball and golf.*

Use your favorite racquet or club, or your hand. Set up to move or hit a particular shot that has been causing you trouble. First, make a few complete motions with your eyes closed. Bring your racquet, hand, or club as far back as you can. Feel the extension before you finish the motion. Repeat this until you have "extended" yourself to the fullest. Now, you can produce a full, graceful motion with your eyes open, and with a ball.

Targeting: *This category includes pitching, bowling, golf, basketball (free throws), kicking a football or soccer ball, boxing, and the martial arts.*

Select the target you want to hit. Now, attempt a complete motion with your eyes closed, with a ball or a sparring partner. Maintain your balance. Do not try a complete motion with your eyes open until you can move in balance with them closed. Feel your errors and correct them. In the beginning, ask an observer to tell you what type of error you made (for example, low to the right, high to the left). If you are a shooter, you can dry-fire with your eyes closed before you actually fire.

Moving: *This category includes running, skating, sailing, swimming, and walking.*

As in targeting the goal here is to maintain balance while being slow and extended. By running, skating, sailing, swiming, or walking with your eyes closed, you can feel your points of imbalance, of tension. You can use an observer as a guide to start you off, but you can correct any errors by first feeling where they are. Moving exercises are a relatively easy way to feel your Rhythm.

Protecting: *This category includes ice-hockey goaltending, soccer goalkeeping, and contact sports.*

The goal here is to improve anticipation. If you can anticipate an opponent's move, you can protect against it. The exercises here may seem odd, but they really work. Have a shooter, kicker, or sparring partner attempt to get past your defense while your eyes are closed. As a safety measure here, make certain that no pucks or balls are aimed at the chest or head, and no real contact made by boxers. If such mistakes are made reverse roles: have the shooters, kickers, or opponents try to shoot, kick, or punch with closed eyes. Focus inwardly, then extend your focus beyond you. Use your internal cues to guide you as you try to "see without seeing." Do this for no more than 10 minutes the first few times. After you have practiced with your eyes closed, try keeping them open. You will see things around you as being much slower, and you will anticipate much better.

Trying to be in Two Places at the Same Time: The Paradox of Being Result-Oriented

BEING result-oriented means preparing to act while thinking and feeling that you have already done so. This is definitely *not* one of the goals you should be aiming for. If you do so, you probably won't accomplish your goal, because your personal time will begin to rush by, speeding from preparation to completion, and bypassing the natural process of progression from one to the other. Eventually, you will tire yourself out and feel less rushed; unfortunately it will then be too late to take advantage of this opportunity or any other until your natural rhythm re-emerges. In sports, only after you have completely blown yourself out of contention will you begin to play well again.

Quite simply, you cannot be in two places at once. You cannot hit a perfect approach shot, a clutch home run, or a target you are aiming at if you are already thinking about the result. If you do not concentrate on your preparation, on yourself, you cannot finish well. Compressing your preparation and result into the same moment forfeits the crucial stage between them—your *Still Point*. When you rush ahead to congratulate yourself, you can only lose. This is the nature of the paradox: the more you focus on the result alone, the less likely you will ever achieve it.

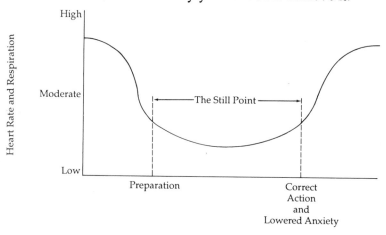

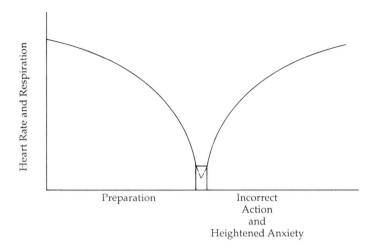

Only in your dreams can you fuse preparation and results, and replay an action if you don't like the way it turned out. In waking time, the process is the important element, and reaching the Still Point ensures the correct process. In turn, the correct process brings the desired result.

BE RHYTHM-ORIENTED, NOT RESULT-ORIENTED. BE CONCERNED WITH THE PROCESS, NOT THE BARRIER.

You can reach your desired result by maintaining your personal Rhythm. Tension and anxiety are lowered, then replaced by the calm decisiveness of the *Still Point*. Rush by this part of your Rhythm and you will certainly know what anxiety feels like, and how it reduces your effectiveness.

A young North American judo champion drew the reigning champion as his opponent in the finals of a major tournament. He had fought this fellow four times in the past, losing each time. Now, however, he wasn't nervous as he had been before each of the previous matches. He felt calm and actually felt he could win. During a point half-way into the match, he suddenly found himself holding his opponent aloft. He seemed to be stuck there. Time slowed to a standstill. He could clearly see the faces of the spectators and the members of his team. He even had the time to say to himself, "I'd better put him down, he's been up there for a while." It seemed to take forever for his opponent to hit the mat. Then, time rushed back and everything began to happen very quickly. His opponent asked him what throw he had used because it all happened too fast to tell. To his opponent, he had moved so fast that he could not be seen or anticipated. To the spectators and judges, he had presented a well-choreographed and elegant dance. To himself, it all took place in super-slow motion.

Seeing the Patterns: Making Predictions

OUR DETERMINATION to predict just about everything—from the outcome of sporting events to what type of car will pass by next—demonstrates part of our emphasis on results instead of process. Because the power of perfect prediction seems beyond us, we try to compress the time between the present and the future, even though it raises our anxiety.

When we are faced with trying to predict what will happen, and if we are anxious about doing it, our perception of time undergoes a radical and rapid shift. First, time assumes the form of a straight line, bridging the present and the future. As we become more anxious, feelings of frustration, of being overly rushed or not being adequately prepared to make a prediction, can take over. To reduce our discomfort, we look for a way to reduce our anxiety. Too often, we attempt to compress the time gap between the present and the future.

STRAIGHT-LINE PREDICTION

Straight-Line Prediction

The Present ——————— The Future

When we use this approach, we lose the flowing connection between present and future events. Try as we might to make one as similar to the other as possible, they are not the same.

We need a better way to reduce anxiety. What happens when we let our Rhythm reflect the flow of time between the present and the future? By understanding this flow, we naturally come to know the web of connections between events taking place in different times. Being in Rhythm is a much superior way to anticipate situations and to take correct action based on this anticipation. It produces a feeling of calm inspiration, not of being hurried or of excitement that quickly turns to doubt.

RHYTHMIC PREDICTION

By compressing the gaps in the flow of time, we hope to lessen the possibility that complicating factors can enter the picture. Unfortunately, in doing so we throw away the true link between present and future, the pattern of events they both form part of.

One successful amateur golfer who turned professional got the idea that by speeding up his swing he could eliminate any distracting thoughts. He managed to change a once graceful and fluid swing into one of cluttered speediness. His game soon fell apart and he left the tour. Trying to eliminate a false problem only eliminates the true process that brings success. When you alter that part of your bio-system that senses time perfectly you destroy your timing.

To be successful in sports and business you must make good predictions and act on them. Speeding up or compressing time just doesn't work: but Believe it or not, slowing down does! Successful hitters slow the ball down so they can see its seams revolving to tell them what kind of pitch they're up against. Boxers see their opponents' moves ahead of time as if they had personally choreographed them. Successful quarterbacks can scan a charging defensive set as if they had all the time in the world, while only a few seconds pass. Successful businesspeople sense the right time to move because they have already "seen" how others will react.

Slowing down allows you the time to "see the pattern" that joins the present moment and one in the future, from seconds away to many months or years away. To slow down is to reach your Still Point. Your time, while slow remains beyond the perception of others. To you, everything seems to slow down, giving you the opportunity to see, appraise, and react to situations before others can react to you.

Personal Time Zones

OUR PERSONAL time zones resemble the speed limits posted by the roadside. Usually we become more acutely aware of one zone when we have moved into another: for example, moving from 100 kmp to 55 mph is experienced as a significant slowing down, even though the difference is only 7.5 mph. Very often our personal time zones are out of synch with the zones around us. When this happens we get speeding tickets, experience jet lag, or get frustrated and angry because we are running late in our appointments.

You have booked a tennis court or tee time, or arranged an important meeting to fit everyone's schedule, and your colleague or partner rushes in anywhere from 5 to 15 minutes late. By this time your game is gone; your temper is rising in tight spirals, you've lost your concentration. Our biosystems are very sensitive to time and its flow, much more so than our wristwatches. Our work time zone is not our play zone, nor are the zones of our family and friends the same. It is a mistake to be in one zone when you should be in another. One advantage of that daily trek to and from work lies in the time it offers us to cross zones—to switch roles from spouse, lover, friend to businessperson, worker, professional. It has been suggested that 40 to 45 minutes, on average, are needed to change zones and identity. (Walter Neff, 1965)

This means that each business day we shift identities at least twice—from say, spouse to worker, then back again—and this process can consume an hour and a half or more. And these changes don't include shifting into other roles, such as companion, wise parent, salesperson, problem-solver, expert, leader, pet trainer, or amateur plumber.

A sense of time and identity also contributes to successful performance. For example, the world's best golfers shape their tournaments and business days around their Rhythm through personal rituals. Their timing begins the second they get out of bed and continues on through holing their final putts. They time their day so that they can drive to the course at a speed they are comfortable with along a familiar route. They make certain there is enough time to practice and re-group before going to the first tee. They know that the Rhythm they establish at the beginning of the day represents the key to making that day a success. They also know the negative consequences of trying to perform without their Rhythm as a guide.

How often have you rushed to get to the course, not had the time to practice, hit a few putts and teed up? Only 4 or 5 holes later did you finally calm down enough to play a game that actually resembled golf. This happens to professionals as well, but rarely to the successful ones. Your sense of timing doesn't begin on the course, the court, the field, or your arrival at work: it is an extension of the Rhythm you create and maintain for the day.

What to do about the friend or colleague whose chronic lateness drives you crazy? I have a good friend like that. He is at least 12 to 20 minutes late for everything. So rather than lose a friend, or destroy my game, I simply tell him that we are booked to play 30 minutes earlier than necessary. If I booked us in at 3:00 p.m., I tell him to arrive at 2:30. That way, I don't get upset, and he's on time. In fact, he is early!

Not only are there variations in the length, real and imagined, of our personal time zones, there is an astonishing variation in the length of the lifetime of organisms and institutions—from the microseconds of atomic particles to the eons of galaxies. The link that ties these extremes together is metabolism, whether of a person, star or gnat.

Let us say that the average lifespan for a person is 74 years, or approximately 648,240 hours; a gnat, on the other hand, lives for less than 12 hours. Yet suppose that the gnat experiences the flow of its life at exactly the same rate we see ours. We see the gnat moving at a speed we can barely perceive, and the gnat sees us as immovable objects. A rainstorm to a gnat might appear as water particles moving at the same rate a glacier does for us. In the gnat's world, time and air would seem almost solid, allowing it is able to walk on air.

All of us have an internal clock that is set to our flow of time, to the rhythm of our lives. Speed up this metabolic clock and our respiration increases, as does the rate at which we perceive images. Slow it down, and respiration decreases, as does the flow of images we attend to.

Was the four minute mile, a physical or psychological time barrier? Some contend that it was largely psychological. Once it was broken, it was broken for others.

Suppose we restage the famous race between the tortoise and the hare, with a few added wrinkles. In their first race, the tortoise and hare are to run for exactly one minute—that is, one minute as each of them perceives it to pass. We know from the earlier race between them that for every minute, as measured by clock time, the tortoise experiences 90 seconds, while the hare perceives only 30 seconds. Now we know that the tortoise will run for 90 seconds and the hare for 30 before each of them stops. How far will each of them run? If it is the same distance, who won?

Race 1:

● ● ● ● ● ● ● ● ● ● ● ● ● ● ●   90 seconds of tortoise time
○ ○ ○ ○ ○ ○ ○ ○ ○ ○ ○ ○ ○ ○ ○   30 seconds of hare time

―――――――――――――――――――

1 minute of actual clock time

In their second race, we'll have them run to a finish line that is set at a distance a fit business executive can run in one minute of actual clock time from a starting line. The hare should reach the finish line in 30 seconds, the tortoise in 90 seconds. The hare was certainly faster, but both of them finished the race.

Race 2:

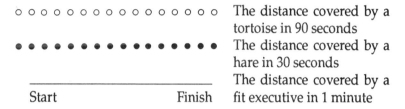

○ ○ ○ ○ ○ ○ ○ ○ ○ ○ ○ ○ ○ ○ ○ ○	The distance covered by a tortoise in 90 seconds
● ● ● ● ● ● ● ● ● ● ● ● ● ● ● ●	The distance covered by a hare in 30 seconds
Start Finish	The distance covered by a fit executive in 1 minute

Now let's imagine that, although the tortoise and hare have been immortalized by their running feats, they have retained their amateur status and work as house painters. The Hare Painting Company is well known for completing a job quickly, if not always neatly, and not taking too much time preparing a house to be painted. The Tortoise Painting Company takes a good deal of time preparing, does an excellent, neat, and clean job, and spends very little time cleaning up afterwards.

Who would you hire?

If you are the kind of person who likes to check on how the work is progressing every few hours or so, you will probably be impressed by the hare's working like mad. But you may not be so enthralled by the tortoises , who are just about to begin after meticulously cleaning, taping, and draping. You might even begin to have your doubts about the tortoises, because nothing seems to be happening. On the other hand, you begin to notice drops and spills on the floor and trim in the room the hares are painting. To save your nerves, you stop checking on their progress, until you notice the hares have finished and are cleaning up. The tortoises are still carefully painting away. The hares continue to clean up; the tortoises continue to paint. Finally, the tortoises finish; they begin rolling up their tarps while the hares are still cleaning up the drops and spills.

Do you prefer rapid workers who have to clean up, or preparers who are slower but don't have to clean up? And what of the quality of their work?

It is unlikely that there are many pure tortoises or hares around, but what if your organization has a number of people or groups working at different rates—and what if their work has to, at some point, come together? You may find that you need a pacemaker!

The Pacemaker

IN THE GOOD old less-complicated days, organizations needed a "linking pin," not a pacemaker. The need was for someone who could successfully mediate between groups—someone who had a foot in each group and was respected by both. Now, a "pacemaker" is required: someone who understands the time streams different groups operate in and knows how to join their streams at just the right points to avoid turbulence and to ensure maximum performance. The pacemaker is the new time-and-motion expert, with a decided difference—the object of study is not how many movements can be performed in a given time, but how to synchronize and harmonize time zones.

The first pacemaker was, and still is, the computer. It set, monitored and could alter the work rate. The second pacemaker will have to be a human being who can balance the person, the machine, and the organization to maximize the potential of each.

The new pacemaker will have to balance a sense of urgency with one of fulfillment, of speed with calmness, of time compression with time expansion. Most importantly, a pacemaker will have to be able to play with time by helping each person and group create a time zone of real involvement—in which activities are not separate, but form a whole that can be productively repeated and enjoyed. He or she will have to understand when it is best for different time zones to intersect, and when to allow them to go on their way again before intersecting in another time, and another.

An organization is most productive when it is attuned to its rhythm—to the rhythms of all its parts. All organizations, all organisms function optimally when their components are in harmony with each other. This is the rhythm of the whole that is created by the interdependence of the parts, not their independence. A good pacemaker is not deceived by a situation in which there are buzzing workers in the land of those who move in slow motion. The pacemaker understands that there is a natural intersection of time zones and paces work to ensure that this meeting takes place.

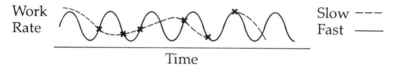

Work
Rate   Slow ---
                                                                      Fast ——

Time

X = points of work synchronization

Using Consultants

ONCE YOU HAVE learned to enter your Still Point and that you can control and trust your entrances and exits, you won't need consultants. I realize this will do little to endear me to consulting firms, but it's true.

Ask yourself, do you need someone to confirm what you have already decided upon? You do, if you made that decision out-of-Rhythm. But do consultants actually confirm? Most consultants sell packaged, low-investment solutions based on analytic, standardized approaches. Is this confirmation? It certainly isn't discovery! Since consulting firms are largely in the business of selling, they tend to use approaches that can create even more analysis and, of course, more problems, so they can apply more analysis— and so on.

Another reason for employing consultants stems from the fact that the most trivial aspects of work or family life (20%) seem to take up most of your time (80%). So, to be successful, even moderately so, you have to adjust your energies and make very good decisions. This is a stressful situation, and a very fatiguing one as well. Consultants have been brought in to expand this valuable time. Yet analytical procedures cannot do this; only you can. You need to be in control of yourself to achieve this. My suggestion, then, is to use consultants in a different way. Use them to work out programs and strategies to cope with the *less important aspects* of your life. Their methods are far better suited to these aspects that the more important, and more complex, ones. Now, you should have at least a bit more "valuable time." And if the recommendations made by consultants in these areas are inappropriate, they can be corrected more easily. This seems like a more natural arrangement; use your Rhythm and Still Point to really expand your "valuable time."

Practice the time exercises below, and you will not only understand your personal time but how to understand and utilize the zones of others.

Playing with Time

FIND A QUIET place to do these exercises at first; as you become more familiar with them, you can do them just about anywhere. All you need is a watch or clock with a sweep second hand—preferably one that is relatively noiseless.

EXERCISE 6:3 *a. When the second hand is at 12, close your eyes. Open your eyes when you feel that 15 seconds have passed. Do not count the seconds; let yourself feel when they have passed! Write down how many seconds have actually passed. Repeat this exercise at least 10 times.*

Now follow the same instructions, but this time open your eyes when you feel 30 seconds have passed.

Again, repeat the same sequence, this time opening your eyes when you feel one minute has passed.

How good a judge of the passage of time are you? Did you

---

underestimate or overestimate the time? Were you more accurate at 15 seconds, 30 seconds, or one minute?

*If you opened your eyes **before** 15 seconds, 30 seconds, or one minute passed, try the relaxation breathing exercises in Chapter 3. Now try the exercises in part (a) again. Keep a record of what happened to your judgment.*

*If you opened your eyes **after** 15 seconds, 30 seconds, or one minute passed, recall some situation that makes you anxious. Now, try the exercises again. Keep a record of what happened to your judgment.*

*If you perceived **less time** than what actually passed, you might find the following experiences familiar: feelings of not having enough time to complete projects; a sense of urgency; feelings of stress; feeling under pressure; working harder but not better; having no time to pay attention to detail; increasing others' anxiety; the desire to make others work faster; the feeling that you are doing all the work; pressure to be a fast starter; or linear, and goal-oriented thinking.*

*If you perceived **more time**, your life may include a reputation for paying attention to detail; a tendency to be persistent, even tenacious; a tendency to go off on tangents; an interest in relationships and good efforts; having things become routine; the feeling that you are a slow starter; the need to fill up the time; or not feeling under pressure.*

The following three exercises are designed to show you how your judgment of time is directly related to how well you can manage yourself. Practice in slowing, stopping, and reversing time will give you another way of experiencing the flexibility of your Still Point, and of managing it.

Slowing

First, do one of the relaxation—breathing exercises in Chapter 3. Now focus on the sweep second hand of your watch or clock. Follow its flow, remaining relaxed for about 30 seconds. Now close your eyes while you tell yourself to relax more deeply, and that as you do the second hand will slow down as well. Open your eyes, focus on the second hand, and slow it down as you relax, as your breathing slows. Control the second hand. Play with it, let it change as your level of relaxation changes. Generally, in about 5 to 10 sessions, spread out over a number of days or weeks, you will see how your inner state is reflected in how you judge the flow of time.

When you feel comfortable playing in this way, test yourself further by letting anxiety-provoking thoughts into the game and noticing how your management of time is affected. By learning how to relax, you will see how anxiety is weakened, and your control is strengthened. Be in synch with the flow of time.

Stopping

When you have become adept at the previous exercise, you might want to go on to this one. Do a relaxation-breathing exercise to prepare yourself. Next, focus on the sweep second hand for about 30 seconds, then close your eyes and tell yourself that the next time the hand approaches 7 (or any other number on the dial that has significance for you), you will try to stop it there *before letting it go on to complete its cycle. You will stop it there each time it approaches 7. Open your eyes, focus on the hand, and center your breathing on slowing it down to almost a standstill at 7. Resume your relaxed breathing and let the hand go on. To master this exercise is to make time an ally—the friend it was in early childhood when days were sweet and long and full of adventure and mishap. After a good deal of practice, you will be able to relax quickly and go directly to slowing and stopping.*

Reversing: REAL MAGIC

With this exercise we are on the fragile and shifting border between magic and science, where those who can manage well will be richly rewarded—for they will not only be able to play with time, but will have more time to do so.

First do a relaxation-breathing exercise to prepare yourself. Then focus on the sweep second hand for about 30 seconds. Now close your eyes and tell yourself that when the hand approaches 7 (again, you should select a number that has significance for you), you will slow it down, stop it, and allow it to go backward. *Open your eyes and cen-*

---

ter your attention and breathing on the hand. As it approaches 7, slow your breathing down to a standstill; concentrate as you "see" the hand slowly move toward the 6, then the 5.

Mastering this exercise will make time not only an ally, but a playing partner as well. This is truly the time we knew in childhood, the one that held suppertime back long enough to finish playing ball, and lengthened the day so we could explore the wonderful world around us.

Be patient, be a good teacher, listen to yourself, and you will learn and understand.

After practicing and eventually mastering these exercises you won't be able to use those old excuses that "there isn't enough time to get things done" or that you are "wasting time". You will have an understanding of your personal time zones, and how best to use them.

7 *Practice*

Enlightment always comes after the road of thinking is blocked.

[*Paul Repo*, Zen flesh, Zen Bones, *p. 89*]

Walking and Transferring

THE LONGEST walk in sports is the one you make from the practice field to the playing field. In the theatre, it is the walk from the wings to center stage. The equivalent walk in business is from your office to the C.E.O.'s; if you are the C.E.O., it is from your sanctuary to the glare of a shareholders' meeting. For a lawyer, the walk can be from preparing a case to facing a judge or a jury.

All these walks can be agonizingly slow and nerve-wracking, even though the distances involved are relatively short. There always seems to be just enough time for your inner demons to be unleashed. By the time you have reached the first tee, the pitching mound, center ice, the baseline, your mark on the stage, or your seat in the board room, you can feel shaken and hollow, and about as confident as a pimply-faced teenager on a first date.

Why do these things happen? You have been preparing and practicing. You should be ready to go into action. So what is the source of these feelings of tension, of being slightly out of control? After all, you have just finished hitting every shot with ease and precision; throwing effort-

132

lessly and accurately; rehearsing until your part has become second nature; or memorizing the facts and stories to run a successful meeting: you should be eager and ready to show what you can do now.

As Joseph Heller might say, "something happened" between the moment you finished practicing and the moment you had to act. Doubts and a distracting inner voice have somehow crept in. Suddenly, parts of your body don't feel quite right. Your club, racquet, shoes, hands, feel different, almost as if they belonged to someone else. Where, in practice, you felt lightness and ease, now you notice a dull heaviness in mind and body. Your mouth feels dry. You are trying to control your appearance and, at least, look calm. Somehow all that practicing didn't get rid of those resistant and irritable demons. You're forced to deal with them when that's the last thing you need to do.

If you recall two of the secrets in Chapter 1, you will understand why you are a little shaky after practice:

1. You have practiced your strengths, not your weaknesses. You have merely (and only slightly) increased your number of lucky hits.

2. To act successfully you must forget the mechanics. You cannot speak well, even in your native language, if you are preoccupied with the rules of grammar.

Most of us practice in the wrong way, and as a result, we may get a little luckier but not much better.

Although the probability of lucky scores changes a bit, the probability of real improvement remains consistently low. A "positive transfer" of both mechanics and feel from practice to the game must take place in order for improvement to come about. The closer you bring your practice to your game, the more efficient is the transfer of skills, thoughts, and feelings. The fewer the elements that the practice and the game have in common, the less likely is the probability of positive transfer from one to the other.

The walk between practice and the game shortens as the

elements between them are more alike, and lengthens as the elements are less alike.

If you would like to practice in a way that brings about improvement, then you will have to learn how to practice. After following the exercises in this book, you are just about there. You need only put on a few final touches. When you do, you could reduce your practice time by about one-third. For your old practice routine, you will substitute a personal ritual that I call True Practice.

You don't change your anger, or your calmness, or your pulse. You control your mind, which controls. You control your body, which controls.

Right action cannot exist and be maintained without a personal ritual to set its Rhythm into motion. Without True Practice, there is no ritual.

Learning, Not Tips

> Don't get enamoured of the "big trick." Don't forget the fundamentals. You may not be as good as others at first, but later it will be so much easier.
> [Peter Vidman, former Captain, U.S. Men's Olympic Gymnastic Team,
> Esquire, May 1987, p. 129]

EXPERIENCED athletes or businesspeople may not be good teachers because they may have no understanding of how they perform so well, and little or no idea of how a beginner feels. But don't be too concerned, there are experts everywhere. These experts often dispense "tips" with great enthusiasm. Tips guaranteed to improve your game, or your business, social, and family life. And most tips are free.

Unfortunately, the tip method cannot help you build a sound and consistent basis for performance. Tips are based on someone else's idea about how the world works. Tips are external bandaids, badly placed. Yet tips have found a receptive and warm home in sports and business. When it comes to sports, sex, and money, people tend to overreact to tips that fit their present situation.

No expert, and certainly no tip, can tell you what is wrong with what you are doing. Only you can make the corrections. Only you can bring your mind and body into synch with one another. It is an exacting but exhilarating process. Any change you make brings with it some conflict, but also carries with it the joy of self-discovery, and a passion for life.

If you want to find scientific reasons for your errors, you have to be willing to take advantage of discoveries, not just of the body, but of the mind as well. There should be no loose pieces, just the simplicity of your inner waves taking you from preparation through concentration and on to action. This kind of learning fosters your appreciation of your lack of separateness from the events in the world. This is not a form of mysticism but a common human state of awareness that has been neglected. Such learning extends beyond the confines of time as measured by a clock. It helps focus you on your inner life, and releases you from the past, present, and future. You and what you want to achieve become inseparable. All time, action, and thoughts blend in the creation of a moment that prepares you to act with integrity and compassion. Solutions appear that were invisible before, old ways of thinking gradually become modified; all of this happens as the conscious mind becomes quiet. Changes now become creative, not destructive — incorporated into your view of yourself, not merely dragged along or tossed aside. This process completes each cycle of your Rhythm with an appropriate action so that a new one can begin. You will find freedom here: the freedom to start a new task, to feel the absence of unnecessary tensions, to do the right thing.

When people are told things which they do not want to hear, they produce or borrow certain standard arguments to enable them to exclude the new information.

You can usefully offset this tendency by remembering that most unfamiliar information is likely to be met by this response.

*Remember, too, that the things which you already know are
mostly facts which would seem to be impossible, unlikely,
or even symptoms of paranoia to a man or woman of
another time or culture.*

*It is this kind of understanding, not emotional reaction,
which will enable you and others to face the truth, and to
learn more.*

[*Idries Shah,* Reflections, *1972, p. 47*]

True Practice: Building Your Ritual

YOU CAN TREAT practice as another plaything or as a way
to a higher level of understanding and performance.

True Practice combines mechanics with your Rhythm.
The maximum levels of positive transfer come about under
these conditions. Blending mechanics with your Rhythm is
the basis of success in both practice and in the game, as
well as in any decision-making situation in your life.

True Practice re-establishes and fine-tunes your Rhythm,
which in turn stabilizes your mechanics. You encounter no
blockages because the anxieties they feed on are absent.
This type of practice is timeless and quieting. When you
leave the practice area, you are excited about the game and
in control of yourself. This makes the walk from practice to
play one of personal power and preparedness.

You take into the game an understanding of yourself, of
what you can do, how and when. This could translate into
such simple yet effective actions as taking one less club because you know how pumped-up you are; trying a
difficult and risky move right from the start because you
know your control is superb; or staying silent until just the
right moment at a meeting where your ideas are being dis-
cussed.

Playing after True Practice gives your game a distinctive
and personal style. It provides you with the opportunity to
win, plus the knowledge of how to take advantage of such
an opportunity. None of this would be there, waiting for
you, unless your Rhythm were there as well.

As I mentioned earlier, practice for most people in-creases their number of lucky moves, but doesn't improve their technique. True Practice is a very different experience. It is not result-oriented. It is concerned with the process. In turn, process shapes the right techniques, the necessary building-blocks of concentration and decision-making. This pattern continues unfolding as concentration and proper decision-making bring about freedom, the absence of anxiety, and the recognition that the time to act has come. This is the mosaic of your Rhythm. It is what you have practiced. It is what maintains your level of perfor-mance, and keeps you from "getting stuck" in the gray zone between preparation and action.

One difference between the ordinary and elite athlete — and between the ordinary and successful businessperson, lawyer, physician, artist, musician, or parent — comes down to nothing more than the training of the uncons-cious. In addition, ordinary people are trapped by a need to show immediate results. A constant state of crisis allows them to rationalize why things have not gone so well. They make a poor decision, carry it out in a tense, hurried way, and become exhausted. Their energies are centered on results without concern for the process. They soon become so result-oriented that they diminish their own natural abilities and strengths. Producing a result, any result, be-comes all-important, and takes them far away from creat-ing their moment to act properly. For such people, practice becomes a meaningless routine.

In contrast, successful people use True Practice as an en-vironment for learning to take place. This process is not passive, but active: you become both teacher and student. The process and the technique are identical and in-separable. Your first True Practice session may cause some conflict because your conscious attitudes may resist the in-trusion of new ways of doing things. The conflict can ap-pear as you first learn to let go, trust yourself, and be in control at the same moment. As you practice, the coopera-tion between your intuition, feelings, intellect, and actions will increase and expand.

You won't be practicing repetitive mechanical movements over and over. You won't just be hitting countless
buckets of balls, or balls propelled by a small, nicely
painted electronic cannon; you won't be attending seemingly endless workshops run by experts. From now on,
you will be able to disregard these forms of practice. As
a result, you won't acquire any new bad habits that can
be extremely hard to change in the future. Instead, you
will be:

1. Creating the right consciousness to go along with the
   right action;

2. Learning about the dynamics of your Rhythm, which
   take you into the game;

3. Concentrating on your breathing, your calmness, your
   Still Point; and

4. Learning how to make the best use of your intuition and
   feelings.

Traditional ways of practicing have produced some unusual outcomes. For example, more records have been
broken in practice than in actual play. This is really not so
surprising, since practices are result-oriented without the
pressures of the game. Also, practice is not a very good
predictor of performance. Many people feel that if they are
doing poorly in practice, their game will be great. They
trust that old sport saying, "don't leave your good shots on
the practice range." How many times have you looked
great in practice and fell apart in the game?
     The mechanical, repetitive type of practice probably
works best when you make it harder on yourself than actual play. But you must realize that any changes or modifi-
cations you make in practice will have a disturbing, hope-
fully temporary, influence on your play. In the case of True
Practice, there are no "worsts." There is only the experience of learning about yourself and assimilating
change, not being hindered by it.

True Practice involves not an endurance contest, but experimentation and inner-directedness. Ideally, such practice, in addition to the four goals mentioned above, should also provide

5. A ritual for priming yourself for actual play;

6. A sense of timing and Rhythm for the day; and

7. A sense that what you are doing in practice is not different from what you will have to do in the game.

The exercises throughout this book were designed with these seven goals in mind. They emphasize self-understanding and control, and finding your personal rituals. Most of the exercises impose conditions that limit your vision so that you will attend to the inside, not the outside. In this way, your thoughts, feelings and movements will form a unity, one that is right for you. These exercises are the basis of True Practice. The movements and feelings you develop through these exercises easily transfer to actual play. You have built your understanding and actions on your natural qualities without the need for the criticisms and methods of others.

Be concerned not so much with yourself but the "self" that stands in your way.

Through True Practice, you have taught yourself not to look up to see where the ball landed before you hit it; not to run before you catch the ball; not to mistime the moment to present your ideas. Instead, you anticipated each move and knew how it would work out. There was no need to look or run too soon. No teacher can tell you what to "see" or "feel." Your own feelings are the translators between mind and body. Listen to what they have to say and use this information: be intuitive, concentrate, stay in Rhythm.

EXERCISE 7:1   *Some Guidelines for Practicing*

Work and play do go together. In fact, they improve each other if each is done with an awareness of your Rhythm. The following guidelines will help you to do just that in whatever activity you prefer.

a. Never hurry to get to practice. Be as slow getting there as you want to feel in your practice. If you rush, it will carry over into your practice. Think of your practice as a personal ritual that includes getting there and leaving.

b. Warm up until you feel your Rhythm forming, and no longer.

c. In the first half of your sessions, carry out each set of movements with your eyes closed, followed by a set with your eyes open.

d. In the second half of your session, carry out each set of movements with your eyes half-closed, followed by a set with your eyes open.

e. In (c) and (d), set yourself a challenge by working on something you are having trouble with.

f. Don't rush; this is your time.

g. Pay attention to the growing presence of your Rhythm. It will tell you when your session is coming to an end. This happens when your Rhythm is firmly in place and you are at peace with yourself. There is no reason to practice any longer.

h. Go out and play as well as you can. Don't rush to get there.

One of the best tests to see if you can keep your Rhythm working for you is to play against someone who has no Rhythm. You can lose to these people even though you are a better player if you don't play within yourself. Stay in your Rhythm and you can only win.

In the early days of the Meiji era, there lived a well-known wrestler called O-nami, Great Waves.

O-nami was immensely strong and knew the art of wrestling. In his private bouts he defeated even his teacher, but in public he was so bashful that his own pupils threw him.

O-nami felt he should go to a Zen master for help. Hakuju, a wandering teacher, was stopping in a little temple nearby, so O-nami went to see him and told him of his trouble.

"Great Waves is your name," the teacher advised, "so stay in this temple tonight. Imagine that you are those billows. You are no longer a wrestler who is afraid. You are those huge waves sweeping everything before them, swallowing all in their path. Do this and you will be the greatest wrestler in the land."

The teacher retired. O-nami sat in meditation trying to imagine himself as waves. He thought of many different things. Then gradually he turned more and more to the feeling of the waves. As the night advanced, the waves became larger and larger. They swept away the flowers in their vases. Even the Buddha in the shrine was inundated. Before dawn, the temple was nothing but the ebb and flow of an immense sea.

In the morning the teacher found O-nami meditating, a faint smile on his face. He patted the wrestler's shoulder; "Now nothing can disturb you," he said. "You are those waves. You will sweep everything before you."

The same day O-nami entered the wrestling contests and won. After that, no one in Japan was able to defeat him.

[Paul Repo, Zen Flesh, Zen Bones, p. 4]

Appendix A

Daily Rating Schedule

ONE WAY YOU can get an idea of the pattern of your Rhythm is to assess your moods. The changes in your moods from day-to-day and from week-to-week reflect your inner Rhythm. By recognizing one, you gain an insight into the other. Make copies of the Daily Rating Schedule and use it at least 2 or 3 times a day for a week or more. Try to do one rating when you get up in the morning, another in the middle of your day, and before you go to sleep. Do you experience the Monday blues, a mid-week energy crisis, or restlessness on Sunday evenings? Using these daily ratings, you can chart the changes and how they influence you and others around you.

PART I

Date: _____ Time: _____

Right now, my general mood is:

GOOD   Very good — 1 2 3 4 5 6 7 8 9 — Not at all good

FLUCTUATING   Very much — 1 2 3 4 5 6 7 8 9 — Not at all

PART II

1 2 3 4 5 6 7 8 9

1. withdrawn		outgoing
2. critical		tolerant
3. depressed		elated
4. perceptive		oblivious
5. desire to be alone		gregarious
6. optimistic		pessimistic
7. communicative		uncommunicative
8. bored		interested
9. relaxed		tense
10. satisfied		frustrated
11. patient		impatient
12. feeling superior		feeling inferior
13. intelligent		dumb
14. lonely		not lonely
15. secure		insecure
16. responsible		irresponsible
17. dependent		independent
18. necessary		unnecessary
19. facetious		serious
20. sexy		unattractive

Write down any special situations that came up today:

TEMPER SCALE

	Almost Never	Some- times	Often	Almost Always
I am quick-tempered.	1	2	3	4
I have a fiery temper.	1	2	3	4
I am a hot-headed person.	1	2	3	4
I get angry when I'm slowed down by others' mistakes.	1	2	3	4
I feel annoyed when I am not recognized for doing good work.	1	2	3	4
I fly off the handle.	1	2	3	4
When I get mad, I say nasty things.	1	2	3	4
It makes me furious when I am criticized in front of others.	1	2	3	4
When I get frustrated, I feel like hitting someone.	1	2	3	4
I feel infuriated when I do a good job and get a poor evaluation.	1	2	3	4

Scoring Instructions

Total up the points (1 to 4) that you score on each item. If you score 17 or 18, you are just about average. A person who scores below 13 is down in the safe zones, perhaps unresponsive to situations that provoke others. A score of 23 or higher puts you up among the hotter heads.

Now, go on to complete the JOB STRESS SURVEY.

JOB STRESS SURVEY

	Number of Occurrences During the Past Month			
1. I have been bothered by fellow workers not doing their job.	0	1	2	3+
2. I've had inadequate support from my supervisor.	0	1	2	3+
3. I've had problems getting along with my co-workers.	0	1	2	3+
4. I've had trouble getting along with my supervisor.	0	1	2	3+
5. I've felt pressed to make critical on-the-spot decisions.	0	1	2	3+
6. I've been bothered by the fact that there aren't enough people to handle the job.	0	1	2	3+
7. I've felt a lack of participation in policy decisions.	0	1	2	3+
8. I've been concerned about my inadequate salary.	0	1	2	3+
9. I've been troubled by a lack of recognition for good work.	0	1	2	3+
10. I've been frustrated by excessive paperwork.	0	1	2	3+

Total Points: _____

Scoring Instructions

To determine how your stress level compares with that of others add up the points that you circled for each. Persons who score between 5 and 7 are about average in how often they experience job-related stress. If you score higher than 8, you may have cause for concern. At 4 or lower, you have a relatively nonstressful job.

NOTE: If you score higher than 20 on the Temper Scale, and if
your score is higher than 9 on the Job Stress Survey,
you've got a dangerous combination going.

Double-digit job stress points to trouble, expecially if your
personality runs high in irritability and temper. Remember the
double-barrelled effect: if your personality makes you anger-
prone, you have to watch out for jobs high in petty irritations.

Use these scales to keep a check on how your temper and
stress levels are changing. Those of you with high scores may be
surprised to know that you have a very good chance of bringing
your scores down, and your inner Rhythm will guide you as you
manage these feelings. Just follow the exercises throughout this
book and you will see how well you can manage.

TIME ANXIETY SCALE

Answer TRUE if the statement is typical of you; if not, answer FALSE.

1. I am often troubled about how
   short life really is.   T   F

2. I seem to be able to get things done on time.   T   F

3. Sometimes I feel that time is running out.   T   F

4. I always make it a point to be on time.   T   F

5. I often regret not having done
   more with my time.   T   F

6. I manage my time pretty well.   T   F

7. It doesn't make me nervous when
   people talk about the future.   T   F

8. Time seems to fly by so rapidly.   T   F

9. I waste a lot of time on things that
   are not important.   T   F

10. Things seem to take longer to get
    done than they should.   T   F

11. I am bothered by people who are not on time.   T   F

12. I feel a constant pressure to get my
    work done on time.   T   F

13. I am frustrated by the lack of time I have.   T   F

14. I don't need deadlines to get things done.   T   F

15. Lately, I tend to daydream more often.   T   F

Scoring Instructions

Each question is scored 1 or 0. The higher your score, the more anxiety about time you have at this moment. The lower your score, the lower your present anxiety. An average score is 7, and most people will score between 5 and 9. Remember, the score only reflects your *present* anxiety. You can use this scale a number of times, and it should be looked at along with your scores on the Temper and Job Stress scales. Higher scores on all three scales indicate that you are going through a rough period. Lower scores indicate less anxiety and more time to do the things you want to do. You can use this scale and the others many times to check on your ability to manage yourself and time.

Question	Question	Question
1. T = 1; F = 0	6. T = 0; F = 1	11. T = 1; F = 0
2. T = 0; F = 1	7. T = 0; F = 1	12. T = 1; F = 0
3. T = 1; F = 0	8. T = 1; F = 0	13. T = 1; F = 0
4. T = 1; F = 0	9. T = 1; F = 0	14. T = 0; F = 1
5. T = 1; F = 0	10. T = 1; F = 0	15. T = 1; F = 0

Appendix B

THE DECISION-MAKING Game is designed to give you (1) the opportunity to use your Rhythm to solve a problem that is facing you right now; and (2) an insight into the pattern of your decision-making. The game can be played using the board design on the following pages. You will need index cards and a pen or pencil to play.

To begin, do one of the slowing-time exercises from Chapter 6. After you have completed the exercise, think about *one* particular problem you would like to resolve. Write that problem down on an index card, and place it on the Problem Box on the game board. Using as many index cards as you need, write down any points that come to mind, one to a card, no matter how irrelevant it may seem. Place these cards on the "In Box" on the board. Take a 5- to 10-minute break.

Now, do one of the breathing exercises from Chapter 3. Select the one that you feel most comfortable with. Before you begin, think about your problem for a few minutes. As soon as you have finished the exercise, write down any thoughts that come to you, and the actions you feel you should take.

Take another break. This time return to the game when you feel the time is right. When you do return, begin with the "Stepping Away" exercise from Chapter 3. Let your attention go where it will.

THE DECISION-MAKING GAME

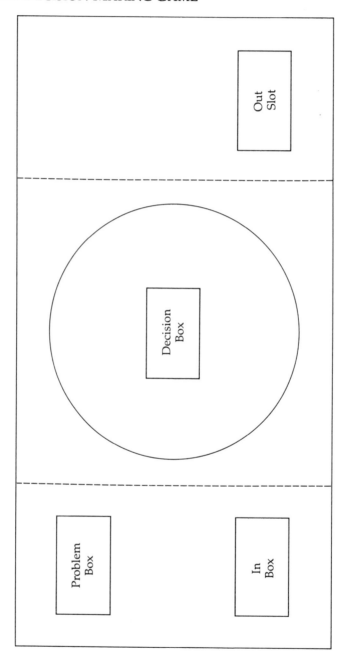

When you have finished, take the cards you have placed on the "In Box" and place them around the rim of the playing circle on the board. Place them in any order that makes sense to you. Don't spend too much time thinking about their sequence. As you look over the cards, remain centered. The cards you feel you can discard should be placed on the "Out Box." The remaining cards can be re-ordered around the circle. Again, don't spend too much time thinking about their sequence. Try to "see" their sequence first before moving them.

Take a short break of 5 to 10 minutes. At the end of this time, do exercise 4:2 from Chapter 4. Now, any points you want to add to those around the circle should be written on cards and placed in sequence. Any cards you want to discard can be removed and placed on the "Out Box."

After another break, the duration of which is up to you, the time has come to do the decision-making exercise (4:1) from Chapter 4. Before doing this exercise, look over the cards around the circle until a pattern emerges. As soon as it does, begin the exercise.

This is it! The decision you reach using this exercise, and the outcome that follows, will be correct for you, and natural. Write down that decision and place it on the "Decision Box."

By looking over the cards in the "Out Box" and around the circle you can see the pattern of your decision-making. You can use this game to further refine your technique and to help others deal with their problems.

We are confronted with insurmountable opportunities.
[Rowes, Barbara, 1979. Book of Quotes. *New York: E. P. Dutton, p.13*]

Appendix C

Capturing Time

PEOPLE HAVE tried for centuries to measure and control time. We have also come up with a variety of descriptions to harness time:

Time Itself is a measure of circular motion with respect to an absolutely non-rotating framework. This means that if there is no such circular motion relative to a stationary reference point, there is no time.

Atomic Time has been used since 1955 and excludes almost all effects on measurement due to inertia.

Absolute Time is thought to be impossible according to the Theory of Relativity.

Basic Universal Time is used by astronomers and navigators and includes the wobble and precession of the Earth's rotation.

Universal Time One is also used by astronomers and navigators but excludes any consideration of wobble.

Biological Time is time seen from your personal frame of reference. It is, in many ways, best described as a "personal sense of time." It is also said to be slower in childhood, slightly faster as we mature, and much faster in our later years. Biological time tends to flow at different rates in relation to different people.

Clock Time is a movement by any mechanical device that can be synchronized to designated periods of time or to a sidereal or solar day (see below).

A Day is measured by one complete dirunal rotation of the Earth. But there are at least two types of days, since the Earth moves around the Sun and around its own axis.

A Sidereal Day is the interval between the position of a certain star directly overhead and when it returns to the same position; this takes 23 hours, 56 minutes, and 3.455 seconds.

A Solar Day is the interval between sunrises on two successive days which takes 24 hours.

Daylight Saving Time works by moving the clock one hour ahead. This is called Summer Time in the U.K., where it was once used year-round from 1967 through 1972.

War Time was used in the U.S. and U.K. during World War II to save electricity and get people to bed earlier. It moved clock time ahead one hour and, coupled with Summer Time, moved it ahead by two hours. This latter became known as "Double Standard Time."

The Week is usually an arbitrary period of time. The word "week" comes from an old High German word meaning to change or turn about. Strangely enough, the week is not a Western convention, nor has it always been restricted to 7 days. Descriptions of the week around the world have ranged from 5 to 10 days.

The Ancient Greeks did not bother with the week, while the Romans started out with an 8-day week (7 in the field and 1 in town) and ended up with 7 to represent the 7 planets (this included a day of rest). Sunday represented the Sun; Monday, the moon; Tuesday, Mars; Wednesday, Mercury; Thursday, Jupiter; Friday, Venus; and Saturday, Saturn. Astrology probably played an important role in designating the days of the week, and in formulating ideas to help people understand the rhythm of life.

In 1792, Laphore changed the 7-day week to a 10-day week to coincide with the development of a decimal calendar. Days were broken down into 10 hours of 100 minutes each, and each minute into 100 seconds. The year of 360 days or 12 months allowed the extra 5 or 6 days to be devoted to recreation. Both the Chinese and Russians tried a 5-day week, with 4 days for work and the 5th a day of freedom. Each month lasted 6 weeks, with an extra day given to holidays. This experiment ended (in the 1940's) when the Gregorian Calendar came back into use again.

The Months and Years

POPE GREGORY XIII was well known for his attempts at playing with time. In 1562 he altered the calendar by having October 4 followed by October 13 causing the vernal equinox fell on March 21 in the following year. How would you feel if 10 days were just taken away from you? What about lost wages? Lifespan projections? On the other hand, you could rest from the 5th through the 12th. By omitting leap days from years ending in "00," unless divisible by 400, and restoring the 10 days, Pope Gregory XIII is largely responsible for our modern calendar.

The cycles of the moon were more important to Muslims than the sun, and they developed a 12 month calendar with 29 or 30 days in each lunar month. The year ranged from 354 to 365 days, but the months had an inconsistent relationship to the changing seasons. This is very different from the flow of time as viewed by Western society. The Egyptians also used the moon as a measure of time. It was once used to predict crops and weather; now we use it to predict fluctuations in the stock market. Egyptian communities held important business meeting at new or full moons to ensure their success. In order to have a calendar that everyone could use, however, the Egyptians turned to the Rhythm of their lives, the Rhythm of the Nile. The annual rising of its waters helped to set the calendar for sowing and harvesting. A Greek calendar based on moon cycles added a month to every other year to overcome the irregularities of the relationship between months and the seasons. This added another 1,050 days for every 70 years. In Greece, the Julian calendar of 12 months, each of 30 days, with 5 days at years' end, made a useful calendar. Although the solar year is not exactly 365 days, the "wandering year," as it has been called, had no impact over one lifetime, and was an accepted measure until Pope Gregory XIII in the 16th century.

Although the sun is still a more widely used guide for time measurement, the moon has its powers as well. Each Jewish month begins with a new moon with a year consisting of 354 days; one month is added each leap year. For Christians, Easter marks the first Sunday after the spring equinox. (If a full moon falls on that Sunday, Easter occurs the following Sunday.)

Time Zones

IN 1880, *Greenwich Mean Time (GMT)* became a worldwide time standard. It is the zone time of the meridian passing through Greenwich, England, which is designated 0° Longitude. Every 15° increment from Greenwich is a *Standard Time Zone*, there are 24 such zones. Every clock in each zone is set to the standard time, which eliminates all local times. Prior to this arrangement, travellers would have to change their clocks at every city they entered, for each county and city set its clock at 12:00 noon when the sun was exactly overhead.

Now changes occur at the *International Date Line* (IDL), where zones in the east meet those from the west in the mid-Pacific at a meridain of 180°—directly opposite Greenwich. A person travelling from east to west gains one day while a traveller going from west to east loses a day.

Other Times

Ephemeris Time in 1956 changed the definition of one second from 1/86,400 of a day to 1/31,556,925,9747 of a year of 365.242199 days.

Mean Solar Time is the average length of a solar day throughout the year. This is a time standard to which clocks and watches are set. To those who possess high-tech cesium quartz crystal watches, this will still turn out to be a rough approximation.

Flex Time: To make your working day more flexible, working shifts have been varied: 8am to 4pm, 9am to 5pm, 10am to 6pm, and so on. Flex time creates the illusion that you have more control of time. Does it lead to more productivity, qualitatively better product and services? The best available answer to these questions is "not necessarily." What flex time accomplishes is to lessen the morning and evening rush hours a bit, but not enough so that anyone really notices. It also adds a whole new series of coffee breaks to the work routine. Probably the best assessment of the impact of flex time could be found in the change in the number of pastries and cups of coffee, tea, and fruit juice consumed.

Sandwich Time is the time of early childhood before you were taught how that odd-looking contraction on the wall "told the time." Waking time was divided into segments bounded on one side by a certain number of sandwiches that could be eaten, and on the other when you were hungry again.

Good Times never last long enough. Too often we feel this time pass as if we were outside and inside of it, simultaneously.

Bad Times invariably last too long, and are felt to be the price we have to pay for the good times.

Time in the Black Hole: Theoretically time slows down until it stops in a Black Hole as neither light nor time can escape.

Bibliography

Boomer, Percy, 1959. *On Learning Golf*. New York: Alfred A. Knopf.

Butler, Robert N., and Myra I. Lewis, 1977. *Aging and Mental Health*. St. Louis: C.V. Mosby.

Fadiman, Clifton (ed.), 1985. *The Little, Brown Book of Anecdotes*. Boston: Little, Brown and Company.

Flower, Joe, May 1987. "Secrets of the Masters." *Esquire*, pp 128-134.

Greyson, Bruce, and Ian Stevenson, 1980. "The Phenomenology of Near-Death Experiences." *American Journal of Psychiatry* 137:10, 1193-1196.

Hutchinson, Horace, 1890. *Golf*. London: Longman's Green.

Kastenbaum, Robert, 1969. "The Foreshortened Life Perspective." Geriatrics 24:126-133.

Leonard, George, May 1987. "Playing for Keeps." *Esquire*, pp. 113-118.

Lonetto, Richard, Marshall, J., Moote, D., and Green, G., 1977. "The Goaltender and Goaltending." *Canadian Hockey Library, Vol. I.* Toronto: LR & Associates Publishing.

Lonetto, Richard, and J. Marshall (ed.), 1977. *Total Hockey: Tam O'Shanter International Hockey Coaches' Symposium*. Toronto: LR & Associated Publishing.

Luchins, Abraham, 1942. Mechanization in Problem Solving: The Effect of Einstellung, *Psychological Monographs* 54: Whole Number 248.

Mascaró, Juan, 1972. *Lamps of Fire*. London: Methuen.

McCallum, Jack, May 1987. "The Mystique Goes On." *Sports Illustrated*.

Neff, Walter S., 1965. "Psychoanalytic Conceptions of the Meaning of Work." *Psychiatry*, 324-333.

Neff, Walter S., 1968. *Work and Human Behaviour*. Chicago: Aldine.

Readings From Scientific American, 1972. *Perception: Mechanism and Models*. San Francisco: W.H. Freeman & Co.

Readings From Scientific American, 1980. *Mind & Behavior*. San Francisco: W.H. Freeman & Co.

Reps, Paul, n.d. *Zen Flesh, Zen Bones*. Garden City, N.Y.: Anchor Books, Doubleday.

Rowan, Roy, 1986. *The Intuitive Manager*. Boston: Little, Brown and Company.

Shah, Idries, 1972. *Caravan of Dreams*. Baltimore, Maryland: Penguin Books.

—,1972. *Reflections*. Baltimore, Maryland: Penguin Books.

—,1973. *Tales of the Dervishes*. St. Albans, Herts, England: Panther.

Thinès, Georges, 1977. *Phenomenology and the Science of Behaviour*. London: George Allen & Unwin.

Travers, Jerome, 1915. *The Winning Shot*. N.Y.: Doubleday.

Watts, Allan, 1973. *Psychotherapy East and West*. New York: Ballantine Books.

Wing, R.L. (transl.), 1986. *The Tao of Power*. Garden City N.Y.: Doubleday.

Further Readings

Barron, Frank, 1969. *Creative Person and Creative Process*. New York: Holt, Rinehart and Winston.

Capra, Fritjof, 1981. *The Tao of Physics*. London: Fontana,

Haber, Robert N. (ed.), 1968. *Contemporary Theory and Research in Visual Perception*. New York: Holt, Rinehart and Winston.

Koestler, Arthur, 1967. *The Act of Creation*. New York: Dell.

Lonetto, Richard and John Marshall, 1974. "The hockey referee: a neglected group for study by sport psychologists." In: *Proceedings of the Sixth Canadian Symposium for Psychomotor Learning & Sport*.

Lonetto, Richard, and David Williams, 1974. "Personality, Behaviour and Output Variables in a Small Group Task Situation: An Examination of Consensual Leader and Nonleader Differences." *Canadian Journal of Behavioural Science* 6:59-74.

Lonetto, Richard, and Lorne Rubenstein, 1979. *An Examination of the Physiological and Psychological Correlates of States of Concentration Achieved by Golfers*. Toronto: Research Institute for the Study of Sport.

Lonetto, Richard, 1982. "The Mental Side of Golf." *Score: Canada's National Golf Magazine*, 97 (September).